The
NOW
HABIT
at WORK

The NOW HABIT at WORK

Perform Optimally,
Maintain Focus,
and Ignite Motivation
in Yourself and Others

Neil A. Fiore, Ph.D.

WILEY

John Wiley & Sons, Inc.

Published by John Wiley & Sons, Inc., Hoboken, New Jersey
Published simultaneously in Canada

For general information on our other products and services or for technical support, please contact our Customer Care Department within the United States at (800) 762-2974, outside the United States at (317) 572-3993 or fax (317) 572-4002.

Wiley also publishes its books in a variety of electronic formats. Some content that appears in print may not be available in electronic books. For more information about Wiley products, visit our web site at www.wiley.com.

Library of Congress Cataloging-in-Publication Data:
Fiore, Neil A.
  The now habit at work: perform optimally, maintain focus, and ignite motivation in yourself and others/Neil A. Fiore.
    p. cm.

  Summary: Increase productivity, efficiency, and full-brain power when you apply Now Habit strategies to your business. What if working harder, stressing more, and putting in more hours aren't the secret to success? What if truly effective managers, entrepreneurs, and businesspeople simply use more of their brain to make creative decisions, work in the zone, and live more fully in the process?

The Now Habit at Work gives you a hands-on manual for building the resilience and focus of champions—the ability to bounce back from set-backs, to believe in yourself, and focus on solving problems rather than seeing only obstacles. This one-of-a-kind program offers
• Tools to enable/inspire superior quality work that creates work-life balance
• Strategies to maintain focus and self-confidence
• Tips to conquer stress through effective time management and goal setting
• Daily exercises to ignite motivation in yourself and others to tackle projects with creativity and ease
Filled with practical examples that are thoroughly tested and easy to implement, The Now Habit at Work strategies will help you increase your productivity while reducing stress and replacing old habits with effective practices. You'll be amazed at how soon your new habits will inspire and motivate those around you to new levels of productivity! (Provided by publisher).

  ISBN 978-0-470-59346-2 (cloth); ISBN 978-0470-88114-9 (ebk);
  ISBN 978-0470-88119-4 (ebk); ISBN 978-0470-88120-0 (ebk)
  1. Self-confidence. 2. Employee motivation. 3. Labor policy. 4. Time management. I. Title.
  BF575.S39F56 2010
  158.7—dc22

                                                                              2010012331

Printed in the United States of America

10 9 8 7 6 5 4 3 2 1

For all my clients who learned to believe in themselves and taught me that positive change is possible even when the odds against it seem insurmountable.

Contents

Introduction xi

Chapter 1

The Seven Essential Strategies 1

Chapter 2

Time and Life Management 15

Chapter 3

The Language of Effective Self-Management 29

Chapter 4

Effective Communications 45

Chapter 5

The Power of Focusing 61

Chapter 6

The Power of a Compelling Mission 69

Chapter 7

Ignite Your Motivation 77

Chapter 8

Effective Goal Setting 91

Chapter 9

Managing Procrastinators and Difficult Employees   107

Conclusion Applications and Fine-Tuning   **125**

Appendix   **149**

Index   **163**

Introduction

Have you ever noticed that work has not inspired many positive songs or books? After "Whistle While You Work" from Disney's *Snow White and the Seven Dwarfs*, you get "Nine to Five" by Dolly Parton, and one of my personal favorites, "Take This Job and Shove It." The all too common message we hear is that work is drudgery and should be avoided. At the same time, we are told to work harder and longer and to accomplish more with fewer workers and resources.

We all could use more positive songs, positive psychology, and positive attitudes for making work easier, faster, and more fun. This book aims to do just that, with strategies for working more effectively, efficiently, and energetically.

I know that it's counterintuitive to think of work as fun, but even when the task is boring, your brain loves to problem-solve. There's something exciting and interesting about the movement of your brain from not knowing to knowing. Why else would you attempt the *New York Times* crossword, work on Sudoku, play chess, read mysteries, or try to learn to dance Salsa?

While some may never think of their job as fun, in this book you'll learn strategies to make any job less of a chore and more of a creative challenge that lights up and involves more of your brain.

Your Choice: Work Effectively or Just Work Harder

If you're familiar with my book, *The Now Habit: A Strategic Plan for Overcoming Procrastination and Enjoying Guilt-Free Play*, you know that I value guilt-free fun as a motivator to start early on high-quality, focused, efficient work.

In spite of my commitment to guilt-free play, I have a very strong work ethic. I have had jobs that were unpleasant and backbreaking (midnight shift at Railway Express unloading boxcars), easy but boring (supermarket checker), and over the last 30 years, fulfilling and creative (therapist, speaker, and author). Regardless of the job, I actually enjoy working, solving problems, and accomplishing something. But I don't believe in working hard or struggling from a limited part of my brain when it's more fun and effective to access the right brain and subconscious genius. I prefer working with my whole brain, shifting from not knowing to knowing something new, and gaining the cooperation of all my resources through effective self-leadership communication.

Caution: This book could change your mind about having to work hard. It even may convince you that you have a natural motivation to work more efficiently and effectively while enjoying your brain's creative problem-solving ability.

Unique for Business Readers

This book brings to you business applications of the exciting research findings in the fields of neuroscience, cognitive behavioral therapy, and peak performance strategies. With these methods, you can take charge of, direct, and integrate "lower brain" reactions, emotions, and energy toward the achievement of your goals.

By applying the effective self-management strategies, you'll achieve in just weeks what usually takes years of expensive training and executive coaching—the ability to observe and manage your usual negative patterns and replace them with optimal solutions.

You'll shorten your learning curve by applying what I've discovered from my own trial-and-error learning and from my work in coaching hundreds of executives, entrepreneurs, and managers.

Early Lessons of a Young Entrepreneur

My experiences in business negotiations and entrepreneurship started very early in life with disadvantages that Malcolm Gladwell, in *Outliers: The Story of Success*, contends turn into advantages later in life. Your experience may be different from mine in the details but similar in the valuable lessons learned.

I was raised in a working-class family in a blue-collar ghetto in Jersey City, New Jersey. I thought every family bought only old used cars and kept extra bald tires in the trunk. It was normal for us.

Coming from a large Italian-American family, one thing we didn't have to worry about was getting enough to eat. Homemade ravioli and fresh fruit and vegetables were plentiful. But even as children, we knew that money was scarce and that whatever food and comforts we had were won by hard work. This was especially so during the years my father was sick, laid off, and then working part-time while incurring mounting medical costs.

When the nuns told us to ask our mothers for 50 cents a week to be in the music teacher's play, I endured pressure and ridicule rather than ask my mom for the money. I couldn't endure the look of sadness on her face whenever I had to ask for something she couldn't afford to give.

My sister, brother, and I learned not to ask for much and to pitch in where we could. We tried to bring in a bit of small change by cashing in soda bottles and by earning tips for helping people who came to the nearby cemetery to plant flowers on their relatives' graves on Memorial Day. We'd fill our watering can and use the tools from my father's garage to help plant their flowers.

George Handley owned a greenhouse and grew and sold plants. He noticed our ragtag group of industrious kids and hatched a plan to cut his costs by recycling the flowerpots. Mr. Handley showed us how to turn the pots upside down and tap them to release the plants without breaking the pots. He then offered to pay us for the various sizes of pots—a quarter of a cent for the smallest, a half cent for the next size, and one cent and two cents for the larger sizes. My brother, sister, cousins, and I eagerly gathered the rescued pots and presented them to Mr. Handley, only to discover that our labors failed to produce much income.

At 11 years of age, I felt disheartened that I had let down my crew and angry that we had not been paid a fair wage. Over the next few months, I conspired with my gang to hoard and stockpile hundreds of flowerpots in my father's garage. As Easter grew near, Mr. Handley's greenhouse was full of lilies, geraniums, and irises, ready for potting. But Mr. Handley's men couldn't find a flowerpot anywhere.

When he finally asked me about our contract to supply him with pots for his flowers, I told him we had plenty of pots but that we wanted double the price, a half penny for the smallest and four cents for the biggest. His workers couldn't keep from laughing as they watched Mr. Handley negotiating with an 11-year-old. Finally, I was able to proudly announce to my team that we had earned $5 apiece, a total of $25.

If you're like me, you may have suffered from some childhood disadvantage that taught you to persevere, overcome obstacles, and pursue your dream. You, like me, may have had a form of dyslexia or attention deficit disorder (ADD) before they diagnosed such things in grammar school. So we who are relatively successful today have learned to turn lemons into lemonade and disadvantages into advantages, to compensate for disabilities, and to develop our own methods of learning and retaining information. It's not unusual to discover that successful people have had to overcome many obstacles on the journey to achieving their goals.

Painful lessons learned early in life are never forgotten and can be used to forge a powerful determination to succeed. You never forget the hard-won business skills that come with persistence and the pride of negotiating a good deal for your people.

What business skills do you have that you may take for granted because they started so early in life and under difficult circumstances?

Unleashing Your True Potential

The Now Habit at Work is not just another book about time management or overcoming procrastination. This book offers CEOs, managers, small-business owners, and work-at-home entrepreneurs—who are already busy and productive—the tools for becoming more efficient, effective, and balanced.

While you may have some problems with procrastination, perfectionism, and feeling overwhelmed, you most likely are the type of person who is already motivated to work hard for your business or your company.

In fact, if you're in business today, you may tend to be a workaholic with too much to do, always working or thinking about work—even on vacation, if you ever take one. And yet, in spite of all your hard work, skill, and intelligence, you may not be as productive as you could be. With so many distractions from calls, text messages, e-mails, and the Internet, there's not enough time in the day to focus on your top priorities and still have time and energy to really enjoy your family, your home, and your passion for music, golf, tennis, or NASCAR.

In this book, I want to give you the effective self-management strategies and tools that will put you in charge of your time and your life. You'll discover that it's possible to work smarter on the projects that really contribute to the bottom line, put in less time, and double your productivity. You'll learn how to access the business mastery skills of producers that permit you to stop procrastinating on living and to perform optimally.

Time Management Quiz

To help you get a sense of what time management skills will benefit you most, take a few minutes to see which of these scenarios fits you. Notice which of these statements best describes your attitude about time and your current time management behavior:

1. You start working on projects early—often the same day—and are rarely late for a flight or a meeting. You decide when to leave so you can anticipate problems and arrive on time. You are seldom anxious about deadlines because you start—at the very least, making some notes—on top-priority tasks almost immediately.

2. You delay starting on projects and often feel rushed and anxious about deadlines, even though you usually meet them. Nevertheless, you wish you had a "little more time" to do them right. You are sometimes late for flights and meetings by a few minutes and arrive breathless and worried.

3. You often feel overwhelmed, out of control about time, and are frequently late on projects and calls. You try to finish one more thing before leaving. You think of yourself as a procrastinator or workaholic who "works best under pressure."

4. You're often frantic about deadlines and are frequently late by more than 30 minutes. You fail to adjust for traffic conditions when planning. You try to juggle several tasks at once and seem to lose sight of the big picture and the essential, top-priority projects.

5. You're unaware of time and refuse to be controlled by time or deadlines. You never think about start times, so deadlines often take you by surprise. You're often late by as much as an hour because you're easily distracted by e-mail, calls, and other projects. It's difficult for you to make the decision to let go of some activity you don't have time for.

Scoring

If you identify with:

#1 and #2: You're doing quite well. But if you feel chronically rushed and anxious about deadlines you'll find that a few time management techniques and some coaching could rapidly lower your anxiety and put you in control of your time.

#3 and #4: You could benefit from adopting a new perspective on time, learning to focus on top priorities, and making some positive changes in your attitude and behavior.

#5: You may initially resist the need to learn time management skills, but no doubt you and those around you suffer the consequences of your difficulty in acknowledging that there's a limited amount of time. Coaching is highly recommended to end denial and to ignite the motivation to learn time management skills that will make your life easier, more productive, and more efficient.

To Improve Time Management and Goal Achievement

- Ask yourself, throughout your day, "When can I start for 15 minutes on my top priority?" Pay particular attention to Chapter 2 on getting started.

- Back-time from your deadline to the present to get three- and four-dimensional views of the path to your goal and ask yourself, "When can I start today?" See Chapters 5 and 8 on overcoming feeling overwhelmed and setting effective goals.

- Schedule plenty of *guilt-free play*. Put into your schedule your sleep, meals, meetings, leisure, and social events. Know that you are not procrastinating on living and thus resenting your work. See Chapter 2 on committing to leisure time and work-life balance.

- Ignite your motivation by creating a sense of expectancy about your future and using your compelling vision to break through inertia and get onto motivation in Chapters 6 and 7.

- Commit to protecting your career, your body, and your life from all toxic substances, habits, fears, and relationships. See Chapters 3 and 4 on effective self-management and executive communication skills.

- Apply the language of effective self-management from Chapter 3 and Managing Procrastinators, Chapter 9, to become a more effective manager of yourself and those employees who need your leadership to overcome procrastination.

Hot Tip

The hot tips offered throughout this book are the result of years of practice and research that could save you a significant amount of time. Mark which ones trigger a response of recognition in you. For example, when you set a time to start on a top-priority project, don't give up if you are distracted by low-priority but seemingly urgent projects. Make note of your favorite distractions and keep fighting to show up and get started in spite of them.

The Seven Essential Strategies

The single most important characteristic of good managers is that they protect their employees—protect their time, protect their dignity, protect their career potential.
—Robert Townsend, Former Director of American Express and Author of *Up the Organization*

The Seven Essential Strategies

I know you're busy, so let me start by giving away the essential secrets for performing optimally at work. Here are seven basic principles for working efficiently while minimizing distracting and destructive habits. While many of these concepts have been around for several millennia, not many know how to access and apply them to work and career situations. With some practice, you'll be able to make these strategies work for you within a few weeks. Start today; challenge your old beliefs, habits, and defaults; and begin to replace them with what has proven to work for peak performers in every field of endeavor.

Principle One

Shift from your current habit to corrective action. The fastest way to change is to link your current behavior to corrective action. In many cases, this can mean doing the opposite of what you're doing now.

Avoid wasting time criticizing what you've done wrong. This only adds emotional trauma to an already confused mental and physical state. Instead, point yourself toward the correct behavior. To be an effective manager of yourself and others replace "Why did you spill the milk?" with "How do we clean it up?"

You're probably a more effective manager than the coach who gave me my first sailing lesson. While our small boat was heeling over and taking on water, he chose that moment to ask,

"Why are you doing that?" I thought that was a really dumb question to ask during an emergency. I realized that if I took the time to do the psychoanalysis necessary to answer that question, we might all drown.

With my mind racing, I decided to take corrective action: I pushed the rudder in the opposite direction and released the main sheet. This immediately righted the boat and taught me that analyzing why I'm doing something wrong or criticizing myself during an emergency is not as effective as doing the opposite of what's not working. Given the ineffectiveness of my sailing coach, I had to become an effective self-manager and instruct my brain to shift to corrective action rather than the distracting and confusing questions "Why are you doing that?" and "What's wrong with you?"

Give yourself corrective actions directing your attention to what you can do now. You'll be problem-solving and feeling effective within 5 seconds. Now that's effective time management!

Principle Two

Shift from struggle to ease: the law of reverse effort. Like many wise principles, this one seems like a no-brainer. But when we think we're fighting to just survive, we tend to repeat what we've done in the past. Think of me, holding onto that rudder for dear life, even while our boat was taking on water.

Struggling is a sign that you're going in the wrong direction. During a seminar at a bank, I made the mistake of handing out finger puzzles—a braided straw tube about five inches long and about an inch in diameter—to everyone, including the bank's president. I instructed my audience to put one finger from each hand into either end of the tube and see what happens when they try to pull their fingers apart. They quickly discovered that the more they struggled to remove their fingers, the more the tube tightens its grip.

I then said, "If you're struggling in life, you're going in the wrong direction. To free yourself, you have to go in the opposite direction—do what is counterintuitive, like facing down the ski slope to gain control over your skis. Stop struggling, push your fingers into the tube, it will loosen, and you'll be free. This is the law of reverse effort."

Following my instructions, everyone got free except the president. He was still struggling harder and harder, causing the tube to tighten its grip. He must have been trained, or brainwashed, to believe: "If you're not succeeding, try harder and put in more time." My heretical advice is "If you're pushing on a door and it doesn't open easily, it's probably a pull-door. Stop pushing and struggling and it will pull open easily. Life has hinged the doors—and most seeming problems—so that they open easily."

In what ways do you struggle unnecessarily and find that you are repeatedly frustrated? Yet you continue to struggle and stay stuck. How will you let go of your struggle, change direction, and free yourself?

Principle Three

Shift from ego-focus to task-focus. One of the fastest ways to increase productivity is to shift in one breath, like a karate shout, to a task-oriented focus.

Categorize your thoughts as belonging in one of two boxes: Box #1 is for thoughts about the past, the future, and what's wrong with you. Box #2 is for thoughts about working on the task.

Students trained to shift rapidly from ego-oriented thoughts, Box #1, to "What do I know now about this question?"—Box #2—significantly improved their scores on SAT, LSAT, and GRE exams. Take any part of ego-oriented thoughts—self-criticism, psychoanalysis, or thoughts about what you should've done in the past or what may happen in the future—and link it to what you can do and what you do know now.

You'll discover that you significantly increase your productivity. As a side benefit, you'll also lessen feelings of depression and anxiety because you're releasing pent-up energies and worries into effective action, giving your brain its own natural serotonin, that feel-good hormone in antidepressants.

Identify your favorite or default Box #1, ego-oriented thought. Practice shifting to Box #2 to focus on the task.

Principle Four

Shift from "I have to finish" to "I choose to start."

Ineffective managers tell their workers that they have to do something they don't want to do, thereby evoking resistance and rebellion. "You have to" means "you don't want to, but I'm forcing you to do it anyway" and "if you don't do it, something awful and painful will happen."

It doesn't take a genius to see that "you have to" is counterproductive and self-sabotaging. It communicates that the workers—in this case, your mind and body—should resist and rebel against something they don't want to do. Yet we continue to speak to ourselves, our children, and our employees in this absurd, self-sabotaging language.

If you repeat, "I have to finish all this stuff" to yourself a dozen times an hour, you'll hypnotize yourself into fatigue, distractions, depression, and procrastination as ways of passively resisting a victim role. For every child saying, "But I don't want to," there's a parent, teacher, or boss saying, "You have to."

You don't have to *want to* do something that's difficult and challenging and could lead to criticism from your boss or clients. But you can *choose to* start for 15 minutes to see what comes to you. Even a simple "I *am* getting a root canal, doing my income tax, taking the state bar exam for the sixth time" is more effective and less ambivalent and depressing than "I have to" do all these difficult and painful things that I don't want to do. You might argue that there are things in life that you have to do that you don't want to, such as surgery and paying income tax. But if you're going to do it, you will find the task much easier when you communicate that you are choosing the difficult or frightening task rather than the consequences of not doing it.

The point is, telling yourself "you have to" will provoke and inner conflict that divide your energies, blocks motivation, and will make this task more difficult and unpleasant.

Catch yourself saying, "I have to," and notice the resistance and distractions that arise. Notice the thoughts that accompany feelings of ambivalence, inner conflict, and avoidance, and see if they include the counterproductive "you have to" message. Then choose to start the task or choose the consequences of not doing it and notice how your energies are free to move forward.

Principle Five

Shift from "finish an overwhelming 1,500-hour project" to "start for 15 minutes." As an effective self-manager of your body and mind, you never tell the workers to finish a task that takes more than a few hours to complete. Your workers must know when, where, and on what to start and when they will be paid and rewarded.

Note that you don't have to keep reminding yourself: "You have to finish." The last time you start is when you'll finish. You don't want to confuse yourself or anyone else by telling them they have to jump into the imaginary future to get to a future deadline. You'll only create anxiety—energy that is stuck trying to solve a problem in the imaginary past or future that doesn't exist except in the virtual reality your mind creates.

Focus your workers on a near deadline of 15 to 30 uninterrupted minutes that is enough to break through inertia and give you a procrastination inoculation shot. Short time frames compete better with all the distractions in your life and allow you to use breaks as rewards to stretch, clear out some papers, or check e-mail and phone messages.

Notice how your brain becomes used to concentrating without interruption for 15 quality minutes and learns to rapidly bring you creative solutions. Notice how focusing on starting in the present moment releases the stuck energy of anxiety and transforms it into excitement and productivity.

Principle Six

Shift from the arrogant, lonely struggle of your separated conscious mind to connect with your larger brain and subconscious genius. One of the most effective ways of doubling your productivity while reducing stress is to access your subconscious genius or night shift mind.

Common expressions such as "I can't remember her name, but it'll come to me," "Let me sleep on it," and "It'll be interesting to see how I solve this problem" indicate that you are relaxing the struggle of your conscious mind and its consciously controlled striated muscles. You're allowing another part of you—your subconscious right brain, autonomic nervous system, and smooth muscles—to do the heavy lifting and bring you a creative solution. In business, we all know of those folks who have brilliant hunches and intuition. They tend to daydream while taking a shower, working out at the gym, or having lunch and come up with inventions, innovative solutions, and creative, out-of-the-box concepts. Like many fictional detectives, they don't struggle like bloodhounds or Scotland Yard to chase after small clues. Instead they typically—like Agatha Christie's Hercule Poirot—"let the little gray cells do the work."

Writers, inventors, scientists, and entrepreneurs have learned to put their struggling conscious minds to sleep so their subconscious night shift can do a little daydreaming and night dreaming to make major breakthroughs and discoveries.

One of my coaching clients took my suggestion to give her chemistry projects to Albert Einstein and Marie Curie, who could continue to work in a room at the back of her brain while she slept. I knew this might work because I completed my doctoral dissertation in one year by delegating to my dreaming, subconscious mind any problems or blocks that arose. Each morning, I awoke with a solution and was eager to start working for 15 to 30 minutes before breakfast to seed my mind with ideas that would germinate while I was at work. I completed my dissertation in 15 hours a week for one year while working a 40-hour-a-week job. And I have completed six books in 15 to 20 hours a week within 18 months, each while working a full-time job. I never told my conscious, ego mind, "You have to finish writing a book." I simply said, "I'm choosing to start at 8 AM for 15 minutes to see what will come to me and to make it easier to start again at 12 noon or at 6 PM."

An Exercise

Part 1

Grasp a bottle, a cup, or a book, and hold it out at shoulder height. Let your extended hand represent a part of your brain separated from the rest. Imagine that this is the way you work all week long: struggling with just your conscious mind, separate from the rest of your brain and body, to deal with your projects. From this position, your separated conscious mind is easily overwhelmed, stressed, and vulnerable to addictions in order to experience some temporary relief from its lonely struggle. Soon you'll be thinking of a thousand-calorie treat because you've suffered and you are convinced that, as the commercial says, "You deserve a break today."

Part 2

Bring your elbow to your side, close to what martial artists call the *hara,* or the place just below the navel where *chi* flows. Now your project and arm are supported by the rest of your body, the chair, and the earth. Notice how much easier it is to work when you are connected to your larger brain and body and the support of chair, the building, and the earth.

Principle Seven

Shift from your default or favorite reaction to choosing to act in a way that is congruent with your higher values and current goals. Your enlightened, human brain is the only brain on the planet that can choose how to act rather than simply react. Think about it: You can choose to get a root canal, pay your income tax, and tackle a new, challenging project. You are more than your "have to" versus "don't want to" voices that keep you stuck in ambivalence and inner conflict. As a human, you have a third option, choice.

To be efficient, your brain performs like a computer to give you your favorites and defaults, but you can choose to override them to fit your current skills, knowledge, challenges, and opportunities. You are not stuck with what first occurs to you out of habit or efficiency.

Remarkably, you can start to break a habit or addiction in 10 to 15 seconds or two to three breaths. Take a few days to just notice the defaults and favorites that come to you when you are stressed or feeling insecure. Are your thoughts about criticism from the boss, escaping to the fast-food cart, looking for a new job, surfing the Internet, or calling a friend? On any given day, 90 percent of such thoughts could be outdated defaults that are not congruent with your current mission, job description, values, and adult capabilities. Many of them are primitive ways of coping with early concerns about survival and acceptance: Will they abandon me if I don't perform well? What if they judge my worth as a person by how perfectly I do this work? What will they think of me if I make a mistake?

Whenever you replace your primitive and outdated defaults with a choice to face fears and self-doubts, you are building your self-leadership credentials with your brain and body. You are acting more consistently in alignment with your truly human abilities and values and, therefore, are more in charge of the direction of your life.

Hot Tip

Keep handy these seven strategies for optimal performance. Notice that each starts with your current behavior and connects it to a corrective, more effective action. Practice focusing on one per day for seven days and discover which ones work best for you in your situation. Then practice one strategy until you can rapidly shift from an old, negative habit to a new, more effective structure that makes life and work easier and more productive for you.

1. Shift from your current habit to corrective action.
2. Shift from struggle to ease: the law of reverse effort.

3. Shift from ego-focus to task-focus.

4. Shift from "I have to finish" to "I choose to start."

5. Shift from "finish an overwhelming 1,500-hour project" to "start for 15 minutes."

6. Shift from the arrogant, lonely struggle of your separated conscious mind to connect with your larger brain and subconscious genius.

7. Shift from your default or favorite reaction to choosing to act in a way that is congruent with your higher values and current goals.

2

Time and Life Management

A journey of a thousand miles begins with a single step.
—Confucius

You no doubt have many accomplishments to your name and resumé, and yet, like many businesspeople, you may not be achieving your true potential because of poor time management skills. This serious drawback in your skill set could lead to workaholism and procrastination on some projects, feeling anxious and guilty, delivering assignments at the last minute, or just not doing your best. Regardless of your strengths, achievements, and skills, if you're busy, multitasking, and overwhelmed, you could benefit from new ways of thinking about time, work, and deadlines.

Set Time Limits to Be Efficient

For businesspeople over the age of 30, the college student's concept of managing time by pulling an all-nighter to complete a project at the last minute is not a strategy for optimal performance. Not only do you need sleep, you also need several nights to engage your dreaming mind in coming up with creative solutions. As an adult, your concepts of time, time limits, and deadlines need to be updated to include coping strategies that are more sophisticated and effective than those of a teenager.

Instead of employing the usual coping strategy of just working harder and longer, and working best under pressure, you can become an effective manager of your time and life when you learn to:

- Start projects immediately
- Manage your to do lists
- Create alternatives to to do lists
- Use deadlines to create three- and four-dimensional paths back to when you start
- Request feedback earlier to overcome perfectionism

Get Things Started—Immediately

One of the first management books I read when I was taking courses toward an MBA was *The Effective Executive* by Peter F. Drucker. He writes that decision making is the specific activity of the executive, but to make the right decisions, you first need to manage your work time and concentrate your focus on the right tasks. I couldn't agree more. The hallmarks of an effective executive are making a risk-benefit analysis, taking responsibility for your decisions, and managing time as a limited resource that must be focused on top priorities. The first decision is what to start on. The second decision is when to start and is a no-brainer if you make it a habit to start immediately—even if you have only five minutes.

Getting something started will give you more information about the project than making to do lists and worrying about getting things done. Getting started will give you a procrastination inoculation shot that begins to break down old avoidant habits and shifts your brain into problem-solving mode. Getting started will seed your brain with ideas that will germinate in the background while you focus on low-priority urgencies and on leisure activities. Getting started now will turn anxiety about the future deadline into excitement and productivity as you release that energy in the only moment you have to be effective.

You might follow the example of very prolific writers such as Sue Grafton, author of the *Kinsey Millhone Alphabet Mysteries*, and Elmore Leonard, author of *Get Shorty* and *Be Cool*. They aim at writing two pages a day. That could be as little as 500 words a day but add up to more than 300 pages in six months. Leonard maintains the discipline of writing two pages before he gets the coffee brewing. Now that would take discipline for me! I use the structure of writing for 30 minutes, coffee in hand, before enjoying breakfast and a shower. I like to feed my brain with ideas that percolate in the background before I feed my body. Then I find that breakthrough concepts come to me while I'm showering and shaving.

Just Keep Starting

Rather than worrying about finishing, just keep starting. The last time you start is when you'll finish. Your new deadline is seeing what you can start in 5, 15, or 30 minutes. Keep telling the workers—your mind and body—when, where, and on what to start, and you'll eliminate ambivalence, inner conflict, and indecision.

Manage Your To Do List

Beware of Having to Get Things Done

When you get into the *now habit* of starting immediately on your top priorities, you'll eliminate the need for making endless

---

Hot Tip

PRACTICE STRATEGIC CRAMMING

Give yourself personal deadlines. See how much you can do in 5, 15, or 30 minutes. Commit to simply exploring a new project for 5 to 10 hours per week to see how much energy and curiosity you feel about it and if you're willing to invest another 5 to 10 hours. But get started. If you want to get it done, get started, now!

---

to do lists and worrying if you're doing the right work and making the right use of your limited time. Be aware of the dangers of spending time on creating to do lists and of telling yourself, "I have so much I have to get done."

1. "Done" and "finish" are in the imagined future, a non-existent place that your body cannot get to. You are left with stuck energy and, therefore, feel anxious as your time-traveling mind is beside yourself in some virtual reality you can't reach. Trying to finish and get things done, instead of getting things started, creates anxiety.

2. To do lists are usually "have to do" lists that evoke resistance, rebellion, and procrastination. The unspoken "have to" part of to do lists says, "You *have to* do this but you don't want to. You should resist, rebel, or at least drag your feet."

3. To do lists are often overwhelming and usually don't indicate the difference between low and high priorities. If you treat all your to do list items with the same level

of urgency, you become a workaholic rather than a top producer who knows how to focus on the top priority, bottom-line work.

4. Creating bigger and better to do lists—as with getting organized and perfectionism—can become a major distraction that seems to justify your avoidance of actually working on a project.

Create Alternative To Do Lists

A fellow member of the National Speakers Association gives seminars to major corporations on the use of to do lists. One evening, while having a take-out dinner with her family, Marion had an allergic reaction that sent her to a hospital emergency room. She nearly died and had to be revived with an injection of Adrenalin. Her next presentation on to do lists opened with that story and the message "I wasn't thinking about my to do list at all. I was thinking about hugging my kids and telling my husband how much I love him. You don't need a to do list for what you value most in life."

Keep Marion's experience in mind, but if you benefit from the structure and organization of to do lists, then you might have four lists. The essential first two do *not* require a written list.

Personal Life

Keep in mind three to five people you need to contact daily— for example, your children and spouse or partner—and your commitment to your body and health, with daily exercise, time for breathing, praying or meditating. You do not need a to do list for these commitments to your loved ones and your own body.

Top-Priority Projects

These are the one to three projects you start on every day. Know when you will start on an AAA priority, followed by AA or BBB. These are the bottom-line activities that will change your life, keep your job, and take 8 to 1,000 hours to complete. You do not need a to do list for these projects, simply a note that asks, "When can I start?"

Low-Priority Tasks

These might include: check on the availability of the conference center, put gas in the car, e-mail the PowerPoint slides to Joan, and call the temp agency to hire an assistant. This is a list to look at *after* you've started on AAA projects. This is also the list of activities you may choose to let go of or delegate to someone else. Keep a to do list for these C-level tasks to clear your mind so you can focus on top priorities, as a reward for getting started, and when you need to take a break from working on your top priority projects. Completing a few low priority tasks can give you a feeling of accomplishment and time to daydream creative solutions for your top priorities.

Free Time/Procrastination List

Make a list of fun activities you can put off until you have free time or are on vacation. They might include learning Italian, Salsa dancing, playing the piano, or writing a book. This is your list of guilt-free play activities you can look forward to. By writing them down in your free time to do list, you free your mind of the pressure to work on them now. You don't have to do these activities now. Feel free to daydream about them and procrastinate on these projects.

Use Your Schedule to Record Commitments

Consider using your daily schedule to record start and leave times and appointments rather than creating an overwhelming additional list of things you have to do. These are commitments that structure your day and allow you to say to yourself and others, "I have a commitment and must stop so I can get there on time."

Hot Tip

USE TIMERS, MUSIC, AND MASSAGE CHAIRS TO TIME YOUR WORK

Music is a great way to ease into a large, overwhelming task. It creates a pleasant, soothing, or energizing atmosphere that makes it easier to get started. I use soothing music when I'm thinking and creating and fast music when I'm typing to create an automatic rhythm.

Timers can also help to limit and keep track of your time worked for, say, 15 minutes. I have a back massager on my chair that works for 15 minutes, and besides relaxing my muscles, it serves as a way of knowing how much I can get started in a time that normally would seem so short.

Use Deadlines to Create a Three- and Four-Dimensional Path Back to When You Start

Time is considered by some to be the fourth dimension and requires a vision beyond your usual two-dimensional view of tasks and goals. If you see tasks in only a two-dimensional plane, you'll be overwhelmed in your effort to jump to the top of the mountain or into the future where the task is completed. This view fails to spread large tasks over distance and time—the third and fourth dimensions.

If you used only the two-dimensional part of your brain, you'd never arrive at the airport or complete a large project on time. You would think about only the deadline or departure time, say, six o'clock. But to be effective in completing your project on time or catching your flight, you must access your right-brain functions to see the path to your goal spread out in three- and four-dimensional manageable steps. You can now back-time from the deadline to give yourself enough time to find your tickets, get to the airport, find the right terminal, pass through the security line, and arrive at your gate well before the doors close at 15 minutes before the departure time.

The same applies to a large project that is due in two months. You can look at your calendar for the next 60 days to make note of holidays, business trips, meetings, calls to clients, and other project deadlines so you don't make the mistake of thinking, "I have 60 days (or eight weeks) to do this project."

When you create a path back from the deadline, spread out over the next few weeks, you may discover that you have only 49 days or seven weeks and only 10 to 15 hours per week to actually work on this top-priority project. That's approximately

70 to 105 hours, which may be adequate for a rough draft if you start today and are able to focus for 10 quality hours this week.

With a clearer sense of how to allocate your limited time you won't feel overwhelmed by trying to jump to a deadline in the distant future. You can now take a project manager's view that allows you to track your progress and focus on when to start in order to reach your weekly goal of 10 hours.

From your project manager's perspective, you now can decide which of several projects deserves your attention now for at least 30 minutes and which ones require feedback before you can proceed further. You now can focus on getting started for 30 minutes on your top priority, knowing you can take a break to deal with other minor tasks. You'll know more about what the project requires within 30 minutes than you know now, and you'll have made sufficient progress within 10 hours this week to know, with greater confidence, what to start on next week.

You'll be focused and can avoid the anxiety and panic caused by trying to tackle 60 days or 100+ hours all at once. Checking in with your third- and fourth-dimension overview or blueprint will keep you on target, on time, and on budget.

Hot Tip

Ask yourself throughout your day: What can I get started for 15 minutes to make it easier for my future self? When you arrive at the task that has been started for you, thank yourself for making today's job much easier.

Get Feedback Early to Overcome Perfectionism

Perfectionist's Myth

> By putting in more time, I'll make the project so perfect that they'll find no errors and praise me, even though I hand it in late. After all, isn't it true that the more time you put into something, the higher the quality of the work? If they believe this, they'll appreciate that I suffered and worked long and hard, and they'll overlook the fact that I missed the deadline.

The truth is that, though your work may be excellent, it can never be perfect. If you tend to be a perfectionist, you'll want to use strategies such as turning in projects before you feel comfortable and including a cover letter that emphasizes "This is a rough draft to show you my progress and to get your feedback so I can incorporate it in the final draft." You'll also need to get over your fear of criticism by becoming less self-critical and by maintaining a more robust sense of worth and self-esteem.

The extra time it takes to attempt to approach perfection often leads to burnout and a failure to deliver on time. At some point, the extra time put into a project yields diminishing returns, and obtaining early feedback about the appropriateness, style, and content of your work can save you time. Getting feedback before the completion of a task demonstrates that you are aware that the needs of the market, the environment, and the client may have changed over the course of the last week, month, and certainly the last year. Delivering early drafts before you gain the luxury of feeling confident that it's so perfect that no one can criticize it will help your clients and upper manager decide what's absolutely necessary, what can be deleted, and what needs more work.

Contractors and engineering firms are proud to advertise that their jobs are on time and on budget. There's nothing more pleasing to you, your team, and your clients than knowing that you put in the work, delivered the job on time, and saved your client big bucks by staying on budget. By applying these strategies of effective time and life management, you can announce that you are the one who can be depended upon to do the right amount of work, deliver it on time, and follow through on projects.

For additional help with time management, see Appendix.

Tips for Making More Time

- Give yourself one extra minute, or drop one last-minute chore, before starting your day.
- Take a 10-minute walk before collapsing in front of the TV.
- Before starting your car, take three deep breaths (about 15 seconds total).
- Honor transitions between projects, calls, and clients with 6 to 12 deep breaths (30 to 60 seconds) as you let go of the last task and get ready to start a new activity.
- Honor the Sabbath or Shabbat by having nothing on your to do list for at least eight hours every weekend.
- Plan two hours for lunch with friends every week.
- Give yourself an extra 30 minutes at the gym.

- Shut the television off early and give yourself an hour to just think.

- Cut one "I have to" from today's to do list. In fact, why not cut "have to" from your inner dialogue?

- Focus on just one thing for at least 15 minutes without interruption.

- Eliminate one stop in your mad dash to accomplish all your chores in one trip.

- Focus your attention for 10 seconds on the external reality of the sky, the clouds, and the trees. Let your attention include something even more real than your worries, fears, and pains.

3

The Language of Effective Self-Management

Catch them doing something right.
　　　　　—Ken Blanchard, *The One Minute Manager*

How you talk to yourself determines most of your feelings and behaviors and your ability to be an effective manager. If, for example, you constantly tell yourself, "I should have finished by now," "I shouldn't have checked my e-mail this morning," "I should be there instead of here," or "I should be like her," you're telling yourself that *what* you did, *where* you are, and *who* you are is inferior to some imagined ideal. After all, "I should be there" communicates the sad message to your brain: "But I'm not in that better place. The place I am in is bad and worse than that better, though imaginary, place."

This negative comparison, repeated dozens of times a day or an hour, usually leads to feelings of depression and anxiety. In addition, the internal language of "should" fails to tell your mind and body—your workers—what to do now, in the reality of today, to actually improve your current situation. Much like "I have to get a lot of things done," "I should" doesn't communicate a leadership message of how and where to direct your energies.

When you eliminate "shoulds" from your inner dialogue, you still can strive for excellence, but now you do it in the real world of what is possible without the frustration of trying to reach a place that doesn't exist. You are more effective because you are facing what is real and can be achieved. You might want to remember Dr. Albert Ellis's statement: "If it should be different it would be. But it's not. This is exactly the way it should be." In other words, save yourself from self-criticism and unnecessary struggle because of the irrational belief that things should be different than they really are. You might just improve your chances of success by dealing with the facts and opportunities of the real world.

Choose to Be Where You Are. Choose Reality

One of my most prized achievements is being voted "Cashier of the Year" by customers at the supermarket where I worked while I was in school. I worked in every department of that supermarket in Jersey City, New Jersey, for 15 to 20 hours a week through high school and college. In my last two years of college, I worked as a cashier. My competition for the title were mostly full-time employees who worked twice as many hours each week as I did, saw twice as many customers, and knew many more customers for as long as 10 to 20 years. I thought I didn't have a chance to win. When customers voted for me instead of the long-term cashiers, I wondered why.

I realized that the full-time employees felt they *had* to be there for the rest of their lives and that their identities were tied to that job. But I was choosing to work at the supermarket only until I graduated from college. My sense of freedom of choice allowed me to greet and serve customers with an attitude of cheerfulness and enthusiasm. For me, it was just a job I did to help me achieve my own goals. My identity was not defined by a part-time job that kept us standing at a cash register eight hours a day. I imagined a very different future, and in the meantime, I was planning my escape.

Watch how your inner language affects your attitude, your energy level, and how others perceive you. Choosing to use your current job to plan your future career will have a positive effect on your attitude. You will no longer feel like a passive victim, a prisoner, or a captive. You'll be planning the right time for your escape or the next step in your career. The military uses this principle to train soldiers to maintain their morale and increase their chances of survival if captured.

Actively choosing to show up at your current job for the next 6 to 12 months will help you stop complaining to others and, more important, to yourself. What a relief! Fellow workers (and your boss) will begin to notice that you once again are part of the team. By freely choosing this job—given your current circumstances and legitimate worries about finances—you can focus on doing your job instead of blaming yourself and others because it isn't your ideal job. As an added bonus, you'll notice that your posture and stance will improve; that round-shouldered, hangdog, depressive shuffle will turn into an assertive, purposeful stride. You now can present yourself to your customers and coworkers as someone who is fully committed to doing a great job and has control over his attitude and life.

Choose Your Job Every Day

If all day long you're saying to yourself, "This job is driving me crazy and making me sick," you may need to quit and find a new job that's more compatible with your personality and skills. But another pesky voice keeps saying, "You can't just quit. You have to keep this job you hate to pay your credit card bills and mortgage and to support your family and keep your health care benefits. Let's face it, you're stuck here."

With this inner conflict going on inside your head throughout the day, like a very depressing mantra, you no doubt will feel less than enthusiastic about your work and your life. It doesn't take long for this form of negative self-hypnosis to lead to difficulty in getting out of bed on Monday morning to face the commute to work. After a while, you might even begin to feel a sense of anxiety on Sunday afternoon that leads to another sleepless night and arriving late for work. At this advanced stage of job dissatisfaction, you may be suffering from a form of battle fatigue that accompanies ongoing stress, depression, and anxiety.

Ironically, though your boss, a hostile work environment, or a boring job may have caused your problem, it is now your own ambivalence that makes you look like the bad employee. Others may see you as a moody procrastinator and a poor performer who shows up late for work and delays completing important projects and returning client calls.

Plan Your Escape

You'd like to tell the boss to "Take this job and shove it," but you can't. You need a strategic plan. You need an escape plan for quitting your job at a time that best suits you.

Consider how much time you need to scale down your expenses, pay off debts, and update your resumé. Pick a specific date, say, 6 to 12 months from today, that's convenient for you financially and career-wise—a date when you can leave this job with a good recommendation. But let's face it, if you're going to show up for work every day—for yourself or your family—to perform at a level that earns you a great exit review, you won't last six months telling yourself, "I hate this job. I have to get out of here." You'll be more effective, and possibly happier, if you consider your own reasons for choosing to stay where you are while planning a better future.

Choice Can Change Your Attitude and Your Behavior

Stop complaining. Once you've decided to start planning your escape—on your terms—take charge of your inner dialogue and start choosing to show up for the job every day.

Remember: A major part of your strategic action plan is to temporarily keep this job to alleviate your worry about bills while you're looking for a better job. Tell your complaining voice: "Thank you and shut up. By next year, we'll be in a better job. I'm making a commitment to stay and show up every day until then." Shift from "I have to do this job that I hate" to "I'm choosing to stay for my own reasons."

Choose to benefit from your job. Since you now are choosing this job—instead of feeling like a prisoner with a life sentence in San Quentin—you can perform it without a sense of ambivalence and victimhood. Peace Corps volunteers live in the same conditions as their native hosts, but each night they can check their passports and know that soon they'll be home. The cheerfulness of temporary workers and part-time student employees also attests to the wisdom of knowing you can always leave a job, you can create your own deadline, and you can have an escape plan ready.

Expect a surprise. Everyone I've coached in this strategy has achieved more than he or she asked for or expected. Today, some work fewer hours for better pay and are doing more of what they love. Learn from their success: after you've started to revise your resumé and have shown up on time for work for a few weeks choosing your job, write down what would make your job more ideal. Rehearse telling your boss what you need to do a superior job. Then work at a level that will earn you a bonus and will allow you to leave the company with some extra money and a glowing evaluation. Then expect, and watch for, the surprise.

Watch Your Language: Push or Pull Motivation

Your internal language establishes your relationship with your-self as oppositional and hostile or cooperative and peaceful. How you talk to yourself will cause ambivalence, stress, and resistance or will integrate your energies to cooperate in achieving your objectives. If you talk to yourself in the language of pressure and threats, you will increase your stress levels and lower your productivity. The opposite is true when you start to communicate understanding and safety from self-threats: You will lower your stress levels and increase your ability to focus, thereby increasing your productivity.

In his management classic, *Theory X and Theory Y*, Douglas McGregor classified companies as Theory X, where the man-agement style is one of pressure and fear, as opposed to Theory Y, where the management style is one of encouragement and motivation. You might translate this dichotomy into the push versus pull methods of motivation and management, starting with effective management of yourself.

If you're pushing yourself, or others, to get to the goal and to complete your to do lists, you're likely to create resistance, rebellion, and even sabotage. Embedded in the Theory X-push method is the cynical belief that you and workers in general are lazy and need a stick to become motivated. But the Theory Y-pull method is more than the proverbial carrot to motivate workers; it's an understanding that you—like all humans—are self-motivated and simply need a safe environment in which to exercise your drive to contribute to the achievement of your team's goals and values. As an effective manager, your Theory Y-pull style of management ignites that natural motivation and calls forth from yourself and your employees innovative ideas, creative solutions, and active participation in making your organization a success.

Which Is More Effective: Asking "Why" or "How"?

Questioning a child or an adult with "Why did you spill the milk?" or "Why did you do the project that way?" can shock that person into confusion while the milk continues to spill and the project remains below par. Telling a child he shouldn't spill milk, or an employee that she should have done the project differently, freezes the release of energy without offering direction. A more effective question might be "What can you do now to clean up the spilled milk?" or "How can we avoid this in the future?"

A more effective manager would tell the employee at least four things he did right for every "See how you can improve this report." That is, to be an effective manager of yourself and others, stop making negative comparisons, link current behavior to a corrective action, and praise all steps taken in the right direction toward your goal.

Catch Yourself Doing Something Right

The author of *The One Minute Manager*, Ken Blanchard, found that employees are inspired and motivated to do good work and are the most receptive to new learning when you "catch them doing something right." You can become a more effective manager of others if you apply this principle. But first apply it to how you talk to yourself. Catch yourself doing something right, and you'll train your brain to continue to produce steps in the right direction. If, however, you have a pattern of beating yourself up and pushing and punishing yourself, you may discover that short bursts of effort are usually followed by procrastination, distractions, and outright self-sabotage.

When talking to yourself and others, you might include the wisdom of Dale Carnegie: "To be an effective leader, begin by praising employees and showing honest appreciation. Let the other person save face when pointing out a mistake by first mentioning your own mistakes. Praise the slightest improvement and offer encouragement."

Choose What Not to Do

NASA's famous credo, Faster, Better, Cheaper, was made into a sign by some creative employee to read, Faster, Better,

Cheaper . . . Choose Two. This provocative statement is a reminder that you can't always get what you want and you can't always do all that you want. Often, you must choose what's possible, given your limited time and resources.

In the real world of limited time and resources, something's got to give. If you want a product fast and better, it won't be cheap; you'll have to invest more capital for high-quality labor and parts. If you want it fast and cheap, you won't get the best quality. If you want it better and cheap, you won't get it fast; you'll have to wait for creative thinking to produce a high-quality product with limited funds. To be a more effective self-manager, you might choose to focus on your top priority, choose when to get started, and commit to staying focused on what's most important before moving to all those other things that are less significant. When you have something important to do, there'll always be something else screaming for attention. Only your commitment to getting started on your top priorities will keep you from getting sidetracked into all the other urgent but less important tasks.

Actions Speak Louder Than Words

> . . . *everything can be taken from a man but one thing: the last of the human freedoms—to choose one's attitude in any given set of circumstances, to choose one's own way.*
> —Viktor Frankl, author of *Man's Search for Meaning*

The words you use when having a conversation with yourself—you know, with that part of your mind that never shuts up—your partner, employees, or children reveal your core beliefs and philosophy of life. But even more powerful and closer to the truth of how you really feel and think are your actions.

In *Emotions Revealed: Recognizing Faces and Feelings to Improve Communication and Emotional Life*, Paul Ekman describes how to determine if people are lying by observing the universal microfacial expressions of anger, disgust, fear, joy, sadness, surprise, and contempt. Even if a person doesn't consciously know that you're lying or trying to cover up your true feelings, she will have a gut reaction that something isn't right. The hidden and often subconscious message embedded in your words, actions, facial expressions, and body movements reflects your true attitude and affects your energy level. Others may subconsciously notice the disconnection between your words and your nonverbal message and sense that you're not telling the whole truth.

We all know how leaders often preach one thing and do the opposite, causing their actions to contradict their words and professed beliefs. Colleagues have said of Viktor Frankl, a Holocaust survivor and founder of logotherapy, that when he advocated that every life has meaning, there was a unity between his words, his actions, and how he lived.

What Metamessages Are You Communicating?

Are your messages and actions integrated around your higher brain and executive self?

You may want to examine how your actions and stated values are aligned with what you consciously and rationally believe. Then ask yourself, "Is my walk congruent with my talk?"

What underlying and overarching beliefs are revealed in the way you talk to yourself and others? What are you communicating to yourself, your children, and your employees about the nature of life? Is it all struggle and sacrifice? Are you telling them, "Life is tough and then you die"? "You have to work harder, but it will never be good enough"? "There is something wrong with you that cannot be fixed"?

Even more powerful than your actual words is the impact of what you think, believe, and expect from yourself and others. Research has repeatedly shown that teachers who are led to believe that certain children have high intelligence scores paid more attention to those children and encouraged them to do their best. As a result, the test scores and behaviors of those children improved significantly, even though these children actually had the lowest intelligence test scores in their class. The teachers' beliefs and expectations influenced their behavior and had real, positive effects on the children they taught. The same is true of your beliefs about yourself and your employees.

Beliefs and expectations influence much more than just your attitude. What you believe affects your brain and body the way a placebo pill—an inert substance presented as effective medicine—improves depression and physical symptoms in as many as 30 percent of patients. You might want to consider, therefore, telling yourself, your children, and your employees that you believe in them and their willingness to learn and do good work and that you are a firm supporter of their worth and truer, higher self. You may find it more effective to communicate to yourself and others that life is an interesting puzzle, a mystery that you were meant to solve and that you have the innate ability to do so. Your words and your actions might communicate that you enjoy your life and are optimistic about your future. Pessimists tend to be more accurate about the odds of success but give up sooner, while optimists keep trying until they come up with a creative solution and are happier. You may want to communicate the metamessage "You're going to make it, even though you don't know how. Something will come to you, and you will pick yourself up and stand on your own two feet. You're going to make it."

Being optimistic is one way to motivate yourself to keep taking another shot at success and face the inevitable challenges of life while hoping to turn lemons into lemonade. An optimistic view of life—and of yourself, your coworkers, and employees—will turn your mind toward what's going well and has the effect of lowering depression. Research by Martin Seligman of the University of Pennsylvania's Positive Psychology Center found that those who wrote down three things that went well each day and their causes every night for one week had a significant increase in happiness and a decrease in depressive symptoms. Remarkably, the participants got so much value out of the exercise that they continued on their own for more than six months, and when tested again, they were found to be even happier. Other research points to the importance of meaning in life—interest in exploring a sense of meaning, doing meaningful work, and seeking a purpose or mission for one's life—as contributing to happiness, healthy self-esteem, and effectiveness.

> ### Hot Tip
>
> What works is not the usual advice of "Just have a positive attitude"—which is extremely difficult if you've lost your job or had a major setback—but encouragement to engage in activities that increase your chances of success and correlate with greater happiness and less depression. Most important, *engage in life*, get up and get out there, and *take action*.

The Language of Stress or Safety: Stop Beating Yourself Up

If there are no external physical threats to your life, then the stress-survival response is being triggered from inside your head by what you are telling yourself. Managers, CEOs, and small-business owners too often blame their jobs for creating their stress symptoms. But most stress is caused by your own internal threats of self-criticism, self-shaming, and a lack of worth if you don't get what you want or if something goes wrong—meaning life didn't go the way you planned on your schedule.

The stress response is a protective reaction that is triggered by messages of danger to your life and your worth. When you send a message that your life and worth are safe, the stress alarm and stress hormones shut off. A message of safety, especially safety within you, is the major way to be stress-free.

When you start making yourself safe with you, regardless of what happens and regardless of what others say, you will significantly reduce stress and the negative effects of excessive stress hormones.

Exercise

1. Notice self-criticism and aim for one hour or one day in which you replace all self-criticism with an apology to yourself: "I'm sorry. I didn't mean to scare you. Your worth is safe with me." Write down your most frequent forms of criticism and the most effective statements to yourself for shutting off a stress reaction.

2. Identify your most frequent "have to" statements. Notice how "have to" can be used to imply "or else something awful will happen," thereby evoking a stress response. Notice if your to do lists—which can become an overwhelming series of obligations—trigger a sense of threat to your worth and cause you stress.

3. Notice how your use of time pressure creates stress. Chronic use of "You have to be in the future to finish, complete, and deliver a project" can cause stress.

4. Notice if your muscles are tight and your breathing is shallow. These are symptoms of a stress response. Tighten your muscles further and take a deep breath then release your muscles and your breath as you float down into the support of the chair and the floor. Exhaling and releasing your muscles will signal your body that it is safe to stop the stress-survival response.

4

Effective Communications

Communication is the ability to motivate, influence, educate, facilitate, persuade, and rally support for your business mission and your personal ideas and goals.
—Tony Alessandra, *The Platinum Rule*

Clear, effective communications are essential for the successful achievement of any organization's objectives. Garbled, misinterpreted communications have repeatedly contributed to the failure of major companies, armies, and nations. Yet many managers, entrepreneurs, and businesspeople think communicating means giving orders, arguing, and defending oneself. Effective communications, however, involve active listening skills, and yet—as the joke goes—a New Yorker's definition of listening is waiting to talk.

Anyone in sales knows that you must listen to your prospective customers to understand their needs, and to maintain long-term customers, you must also walk in their shoes, in their words, rhythms, and tone. In other words, successful businesses are based on long-term relationships in which you connect with your customers. You achieve this special connection by providing outstanding service and by demonstrating that you've heard them and can empathize with their pain, hopes, and aspirations. That level of listening takes you beyond arguing or debating to a deep, felt sense of being heard, accepted, and connected with a fellow human being. This deep connection is based on effective communication that forges loyalty among teammates, employees and customers.

Effective versus Ineffective Communications

- Ineffective communication involves debating another for the purpose of defeating the person or removing opposition to your own goals and perspective. It's based on a win-lose model of relationships. This style of "communication" stems from a model of the world that is split into right-wrong, win-lose, or good-bad without any middle ground. There's only one right way and, therefore, no respect for, or inclusion of, the differing views and experiences of others that could enrich our knowledge of the world and yield a more accurate model; instead, we repeatedly argue for our own limited perspective. Success is marked by a break in the conflict, as the defeated person temporarily retreats. Friction, however, usually continues, resulting in resistance, loss of team effectiveness, and often some form of sabotage until there's a return of a balance of power and respect.

- Effective communication, on the other hand, aims to understand the other's perspective, feelings, and message. When both parties can hear the perspective of the other, there's a win-win based on mutual understanding and respect that often leads to cooperation, interdependence, and customer loyalty. Success is achieved when the speaker says, "Yes, that's what I mean. You understand me."

Effective communication skills allow for the coexistence of differences—the higher cognitive ability to hold a paradox and accept the gray area that is the middle ground or golden mean. Rather than trying to win a debate about who's right and who's wrong, the goal of effective communication is to build and maintain connection, support, and a working relationship that is mutually beneficial and, therefore, long-lasting.

Demonstrating a willingness to listen to and understand the other's perspective and experience (without negating the right to your point of view) provides a sense of safety and acceptance that improves your chances of negotiating a successful contract or a sale.

The Power of Active Listening

The power of active listening really shows itself in the customer service department—formerly called the complaint department—and when negotiating contracts. The companies that have the best customer service departments have fewer complaints, more satisfied customers, and more repeat business. These are companies that train their people in the essential communication skill of listening to, rather than arguing with, customers.

Properly trained customer service personnel focus on listening, making sure the customer feels heard, correcting the problem, and delivering superior service to create a satisfied customer. They learn to avoid arguing about who's right and who's telling the truth.

My effective communication skills workshop includes a listening exercise in which one person role-plays an employee or customer and the other listens in the role of manager or customer service personnel. The initial goal is to listen for at least three sentences before paraphrasing what is said until the speaker agrees that he or she was heard and understood. Once the participants demonstrate an understanding of the upset or angry customer, the customers become more reasonable. One actual customer said, "Oh, you're so nice. I thought you were going to argue with me and accuse me of lying."

During one session with a group of engineers from a construction company, the engineers interrupted and started debating and problem-solving before the subordinate could finish a sentence. Even in a role-played confrontation, the discussions got quite heated because it's so frustrating when someone doesn't listen when you're trying to communicate feelings of anger and hurt about a perceived violation of your rights and dignity.

It took several days of practice before the construction company engineers and managers were able to listen to 10 sentences without interrupting. At that point they were able to accurately paraphrase what the speaker was trying to communicate. By then, several members of this mostly male audience whispered to me during breaks, "This listening stuff really works at home with my wife." To which I replied, "If you want to be even more effective try saying, 'Tell me more' and 'You're right.'"

It's only natural that active listening would work in personal relationships as well as customer service, human resources, and employee supervision. After all, listening so intently to others that you can paraphrase their words and feelings leaves no time to prepare a debate in your head, to judge them, or to defend your position. This total attention to what they're saying communicates acceptance and allows the speaker to feel comfortable in revealing more. In business, this means satisfied customers, repeat business, and more sales. Effective communication skills link directly to the bottom line of any business.

Effective Communication Exercise

The participants in my training groups have found that the more sensitive the topic and the more heated the discussion, the more they needed to follow the guidelines for achieving satisfactory communications. They have learned that the process of accurate and active listening flows more naturally after using these guidelines once or twice:

1. Schedule a time when the two of you can talk without interruption.

2. Face each other so that you are able to observe facial expressions and body language. Leave enough room between you to be comfortable; experiment with three to four feet of space. Avoid placing any furniture between you.

3. Decide who will speak first. While one speaks, the other actively listens and observes. The listener concentrates on the speaker's words, tone of voice, and body language, in order to be able to paraphrase the total message. The speaker stops after three to five sentences or after one complete idea—just enough time for the listener to grasp the meaning and short enough to permit easy paraphrasing.

4. The listener paraphrases the words and observable expressions of the speaker, without interpretation or correction. If the speaker is going too fast, the listener can interrupt and say, "Wait a minute. Let me see if I understand what you've said so far."

5. After the listener has paraphrased the words, the speaker points out where the listener was accurate, corrects any

miscommunication, and shares any insights gained from hearing how his or her verbal and nonverbal message was perceived.

6. The process continues until the first speaker is finished and satisfied that he or she feels understood. Then the speaker and listener change roles (changing seats would be a good idea, too) and repeat the process until the second speaker has completed his or her message.

Paraphrasing requires careful attention to the speaker's words, tone, and physical messages, as well as to the selection of words that capture the feeling and meaning of the communication. The objective is to feed back to the speaker the essence of what was communicated verbally and nonverbally. Paraphrasing serves the following purposes:

- It focuses the listener's attention on the speaker rather than on judging, debating, or seeking solutions.

- It conveys to the speaker respect and a sincere effort to try to understand.

- It provides the listener with a check on the accuracy of his or her perceptions.

- It assists the speaker in clarifying the meaning, as well as exploring new meanings, of the feelings communicated. An example of paraphrasing for this purpose would be: "Your words stated that you feel hurt, but your tone of voice and clenched fist make me wonder if you're also angry."

After you've followed the guidelines at least once, use them flexibly but stick to the essence of listening to each other rather than debating. Companies that have used active listening skills have been amazed at how helpful they can be in unraveling intricate blocks to communications, negotiations, and productive teamwork.

Communication Guidelines

You Are Always Communicating

To ensure that your silence or body language is not misinterpreted, you may need to communicate how you're feeling physically and emotionally.

> "If I seem a little distracted, it's not you; it's just that I've got an awful cold."

> "I'm finding it difficult to tell you how I feel because I'm afraid it will damage our relationship, but I'm really angry that you didn't support me in the meeting."

The Message Sent Is Not Always the Message Heard

Avoid negative assumptions about the other's character or intention, and ask for clarification when in doubt about the meaning of the message or action.

> "I think I know what you mean, but let me paraphrase to make sure."

> "Maybe I made a mistake in writing down the date of our meeting. I was expecting you at 9 AM this morning."

Communication Is Not Complete Until the Recipient Acknowledges the Message

> Person A: It's a beautiful day, isn't it?
>
> Person B: Yes, it is. I'm looking forward to a long walk in the park.

As opposed to:

> Person A: It's a beautiful day, isn't it?
>
> Person B: Did you see the Laker's game last night?

The Speaker Is Responsible for Ensuring the Recipient Understands

Walk a mile in his or her moccasins. Attempt to empathize with the recipient's culture and frame of reference. Pay attention to differences in language and meaning.

> "You seem puzzled. Maybe I wasn't being clear?"
>
> "Excuse me, I want to make sure you understand what I mean. Let me say it a different way."

Use "I" Statements

Stick to your subjective truth, your problem, and what you would like to achieve. For example,

> "I have a problem: I'm trying to support your career development but am disappointed when you come in late and fail to deliver on your projects."

Avoid mind reading, analyzing, and dictating to the other. Avoid saying,

"You should stop being so negative. You're *always* late (or forgetful, or too sensitive)."

Avoid sarcasm or kidding during a serious discussion. Acknowledge hurt, anger, or discouragement directly with an "I" statement. For example,

"I don't care for sarcasm. If you're angry, tell me directly and stop telling me I can't take a joke and that I'm too sensitive."

No Cross-Complaining

Communication is most effective when focused on one speaker or issue at a time. This requires nondefensive listening. The initiator of a complaint needs to be

- Heard
- Understood
- Satisfied that an agreement addresses the issue before the other person responds by paraphrasing and possibly clarifying

Schedule Cool-Down Periods and Times for Expressing Emotion

When arguments become circular, attempts to communicate should be stopped and a cooling off period agreed upon.

"Is this a good time for you to talk? Would tonight at nine be better?"

Communication Styles and Preferences Differ

The failure of communication has many causes. Certainly, one major cause is simply that we're all different, with different styles of communication and with preferences for how we like to receive our communications. Diversity of styles, cultures, and preferences is a fact, not a problem. It is essential for any businessperson to have executive-level communication skills and an understanding of the differing styles and preferences of customers, suppliers, and staff.

Personality styles and communication preferences can be placed on two axes: direct versus indirect and task-oriented versus people-oriented.

The four types of communication and personality styles can be divided into:

1. Direct and task-oriented: the CEO, managers, and directors

2. Direct and people-oriented: sales and public relations

3. Indirect and task-oriented: accounting and technical staff

4. Indirect and people-oriented: human resources (HR) and administrative personnel

Regardless of the organization, almost every team must have: a director type who is the CEO, president, or manager;

sales or public relations types; task-oriented accounting and technical staff; and HR or administrative professionals who are more people-oriented. (See Figure 4.1.)

These categories are general, and in the real world, traits, styles, and communication preferences overlap and combine. But this diagram will help you better grasp the fact that the people in your office or business have diverse communication styles, needs, and preferences. Keep in mind that diversity is a fact, not a problem.

Learning Styles

In addition to different styles of communicating, your employees, partners, and customers have different learning styles that influence how they see, hear, and feel what you're presenting. One of the experts in communicating complex plans is the former head football coach for the Oakland Raiders, John Madden. This master coach once said: "With some players you just have to tell them the play and they've got it. Others, you have to tell it to them and draw it on the board. And for some, you need to tell them the play, draw it on the board, and they don't really get it until they run it through on the field."

What head coach Madden knew and learned—he holds a master's degree in education and at age 42 was the youngest coach ever to reach 100 regular season victories—is that some people learn primarily by hearing (aurally), others by seeing (visually), and still others physically (kinesthetically).

To effectively train and communicate with your employees, it's useful to know their primary way of learning so they *hear* you and feel heard, clearly *see* what you mean, and *grasp*

	Task-oriented	People-oriented
Direct	Assertive; decision maker; risk taker; one-way communication; high achiever; talkative; gives orders **Style**: likes clear, brief, bulleted memos; time conscious: "Don't waste my time. When can you get that report to me?" **Needs:** direct, brief, task-relevant information **Job title**: CEO, COO, Director, President	Persuasive; outgoing; negotiator; talkative; dreamer; big concepts; optimistic; confident; enthusiastic **Style**: likes open and friendly talk and praise and encouragement: "This is a terrific challenge and opportunity. We can do it." **Needs**: recognition, freedom of expression, a challenging activity **Job title**: Sales, Public Relations
Indirect	Risk-avoidant; thorough; adheres to the rules; factual and meticulous; neat; diplomatic; high standards; accurate **Style**: likes facts without a lot of personal information or questions: "Just give me the facts. Would you mind telling me what these charges were for?" **Needs**: accuracy, organization, formal interactions **Job title**: Accountant, Engineer, Computer Technician, IT	Friendly, calm, good listener, patient; sincere; team player; likes to focus on one activity at a time **Style**: likes warm, friendly, accepting, non-confrontational talk: "Good morning. How are you feeling?" "How can I help?" **Needs**: a friendly, casual environment, to feel appreciated, any details need to be in writing **Job title**: Human Resources; Social Worker; Administrative Professional

FIGURE 4.1 Four Major Communication Styles at Work

what you want to convey. If you closely listen to and observe your customers and employees, you'll discover that they use words that signal their favorite ways of perceiving and grasping new information. Auditory people are listening to the sound and tone of your voice and want to be heard. They are very sensitive to the emotions conveyed by the tone and pitch of voice. Visual types have to see the words, and it's not clear to them until you draw them a picture. Kinesthetic types must physically and emotionally feel what you're talking about so they can get a handle on it and grasp it.

Take a few days to notice which words signal to salespeople your primary way of learning and receiving communications. Also notice how your top salespeople adjust to the preferred communication and learning style of their customers.

These often overlooked skills will significantly improve your business relationships, resolve conflicts more quickly, and make you a more effective manager.

5

The Power of Focusing

It's easy to have faith in yourself and have discipline when you're a winner, when you're number one. What you've got to have [to be a champion] is faith and discipline when you're not yet a winner.

—Vince Lombardi, Football Hall-of-Fame Coach

One Sunday afternoon, Ellen, in search of interesting subjects to photograph, came upon a young man dressed in leather standing next to his motorcycle. When she asked if she could take his picture, the young man snapped open a switchblade in her face and shouted, "Is this what you want to see, lady?" Ellen was so focused on taking his photo that—without experiencing any fear—she reached for the hand holding the knife and said, "Yes, would you tilt it like this so it reflects the sun?"

At her job, Ellen was the one who seemed to be brandishing the switchblade. She had been angry at her boss for months because he refused to promote her to supervise an all-male department. Each morning she would shoot daggers at him because of his prejudice, and she started procrastinating on key projects and coming to work late.

She was even angrier at herself because she had lost control over her behavior, which was now validating her boss's opinion of her. But her experience of focusing on getting that gorgeous photo—regardless of fear or intimidation—helped her solve her problem with her boss.

I simply pointed out to Ellen that when she focused on a goal, such as taking that photo, she refused to be defined as the enemy or the problem. She in fact acted as if her biker would cooperate and help her achieve her goal. And he did. He posed for half a dozen photos. She simply had to apply that focus on her goal with her boss and refuse to accept that they had to be enemies.

The next day Ellen's boss glared at her as usual, expecting that she'd give him the shooting-daggers look. But he had a surprise coming, because she simply smiled and said, "Good morning." The poor guy didn't know what hit him. His former problem employee was now smiling and showing up on time. His negative expectation that Ellen would a problem had no real enemy to fight with. It takes two to maintain tension in a tug-of-war, and Ellen was no longer playing that game. It took a few more friendly, nonthreatening exchanges, but, within three months Ellen became the first woman supervisor of her department.

Such is the power of focusing so intently and persistently on your goal that others feel compelled to cooperate with your vision. This is the answer to the question "How do people take charge of their lives and wind up doing what they want?" They focus—in spite of distractions, fears, and setbacks and not necessarily with willpower or great courage—with an almost obsessive interest, curiosity, and passion. Often they write out their goals and mission statement so it becomes a clear, compelling, magnetic path that pulls them forward whenever there's the possibility of being sidetracked. Just as you repeatedly check your map or global positioning system (GPS) to stay on course, you can check in with your mission statement to stay on the path to your goal.

Creating a Magnetic Vision

To maintain their focus on their missions, fighter pilots in World War II would leave an apple half eaten, a letter unread, or a detective mystery unsolved. They knew that with all the

Hot Tip

The following tips will help you achieve optimal performance.

☐ Focus on just doing the job, shifting in one breath from self-criticism and judging your worth.

☐ Focus on what the task requires now, not on trying to fix the past or control the future.

☐ Focus on achieving human excellence, not on perfection.

☐ Focus on doing what you can do now, not comparing yourself to another person or on what you think you should be able to do if the circumstances were ideal.

☐ Focus on difficult events and people as facts that you can coexist with, not as problems, obstacles, or enemies that you need to solve, avoid, or fight.

☐ Focus on how to clean up the spilled milk, not on why you spilled the milk.

☐ Focus on maintaining a sense of self worth that is safe from judgment rather than allowing your worth as a person to be determined by anyone's opinion of your work or your net worth.

missions they had to fly, they would be tired, stressed, and on the verge of panic at the sight of each new enemy plane. They knew of the temptation to give in to depressive thoughts, weariness, and the wish that it would soon be over. They also knew that if they had something to look forward to, something to complete, their minds could home in on that thought and arouse a little more motivation to face one more dogfight, survive the loss of one more buddy, and get through one more mission.

Try this exercise to improve your own focus on your mission and the path to your goals and to identify the distractions that could pull you off course. Imagine that you are driving at night on a six-lane highway, with three lanes on your side.

1. The high beams from oncoming traffic are shining in your eyes. Where do you focus? Do you look at the driver and curse?

2. Now you're in the middle lane, and it starts to rain. Large trucks are passing you on the left and the right, spraying water across your windshield. Where do you focus your attention?

3. Do you look at what could go wrong or do you focus in the direction you want to go? Identify your default or favorite reactions when you are under pressure. First, just notice where your mind goes and what thoughts and feelings come to you. Learn to recognize your favorite thoughts and distractions as outdated habits that no longer have control over you.

4. Then practice using a compelling, magnetic mission— your image of how you wish to live and work, using more of your brain and skills—to pull your mind's attention and your body into your lane, headed toward your destination.

This exercise will improve your concentration on major, overwhelming projects, as well as your golf or tennis game. It has helped me ski better on slalom racecourses. If you've ever skied down a slalom course at breakneck speed, you know you have to focus downhill at the track around the poles ahead. If you allow yourself to be distracted by each pole as you approach it, you will lose sight of your mission and most likely go flying into the orange netting off to the side. Then you might suffer, as I have, the taunts of ski club buddies calling you a tuna because you've been netted.

To perform optimally know what distracts you and know how to instantly refocus on your compelling, magnetic mission. Practice this exercise in both your work and play settings, and you will quickly improve your ability to stay focused on your mission and achieve your goals.

6

The Power of a Compelling Mission

Leaders can conceive and articulate goals that lift people out of their petty preoccupations and unite them in pursuit of objectives worthy of their best efforts.

—John Gardner

To help you create an overarching sense of mission that could improve your work efficiency, I've listed some of my mission statements and vision as examples. Because of my years of experience working with hundreds of procrastinators as well as high-level achievers, I've learned to quickly identify inner conflict, ambivalence, and the distractions that most frequently pull me off course. And I've trained myself to shift, in just a few breaths, to my executive brain ability to choose to focus on a high priority project and to recommit to my leadership vision.

Over the years, I've taught others how to rapidly shift from stress to safety and from anxiety about the future to what they can do now—using the symptom to trigger the solution. The fastest way to change negative patterns to productive, healthy habits is to use your awareness of negative habits to alert you to shift to corrective actions. You'll develop healthy habits more quickly when they follow from your values and mission statements. Listed here are examples you may wish to adapt to your unique situation and your unique personality.

(Note that here *I* means "my executive brain and strongest self" in its proper leadership and protective roles, as opposed to any frightened, primitive, or outdated identities.)

- *I* manage my life from choice. *I* refuse to stay stuck in inner conflict between the voices of "you have to" and "I don't want to."
- *I* limit my stress reaction to less than 30 seconds. *I* replace threats with safety. My worth is safe with me.

- *I* am committed to accepting reality rather than fighting against it. *I* stay focused in the reality of the present moment, bringing my mind in from the imagery past and future.

- *I* take at least three deep breaths before starting to work in order to connect with more of my brain-cell power. *I* stop my conscious mind and ego from struggling as if separate from my larger brain and self.

- *I* integrate every part of me into a powerful, focused team. *I* answer the "what if" questions of my worrying mind and bring all parts together around my mission. [See the Conclusion for how to respond to the worrying mind's "what if" questions.]

- *I* continue to play each moment of the game, commit to each step of the race, regardless of the score, the odds, or the belief of others that I've already lost.

- *I*, acting from my higher, executive brain, am in charge of my life, not my lower-brain survival functions.

- *I* start my day with 30 minutes of quality, uninterrupted work on my top priority.

- *I* am committed to living in inner peace with compassion for, and acceptance of, all human beings, including myself.

Notice which examples of mission statements are the most aligned with your values and goals. Adapt them to one sentence that quickly focuses your attention on how to effectively manage your career and business goals. Experiment with an overarching statement such as "I am committed to living in inner peace" for one week and see how it affects your stress level and your customer relations. Then try another statement such as "I live my life from choice" to see how it helps you minimize procrastination, perform optimally, and keep true to your life mission and daily goals.

Write Your Own Mission Statements and Commitments to Yourself

As you clarify your mission statement, you'll be energizing your brain to play a leadership and coaching role that unites all parts of you—cognitive, emotional, and psychological—into a team focused on achieving your goals.

_____

_____

_____

_____

_____

_____

_____

_____

_____

_____

_____

_____

_____

_____

_____

Focused in One Breath: Leadership Mission, Vision, and Focus

Exercise: Focused in One Breath

Use this exercise to train yourself to become focused within the time it takes to complete one to three full breaths. Do this exercise every time you notice self-criticism, worry, or frustration, several times a day, and in one to two weeks, you'll significantly shorten the time you spend distracted from your higher vision.

1. The next time you find yourself tightening your fists or your jaw, furrowing your brow, or starting to curse because something isn't going your way, inhale and consciously tighten your muscles further. Then hold the tension and your breath for a few more seconds before exhaling completely and floating down into your chair, the soles of your feet, and the earth or the floor. (*Note:* A good time to practice this is when you're stuck in traffic to calm yourself before you arrive at work or for a meeting.)

2. When you exhale, open your hands as if to say, "It's out of my hands. This is going to be interesting because I'm clearly not in control of this situation." (*Note:* Practice this with your children, your parents, your boss, or your employees.)

3. Give yourself 15 to 20 seconds to hold your breath and exhale at least three times. With each exhalation, let go of more tension, and focus your attention on choosing to face the task before you as simply a fact of life, rather

than taking it personally or making it a problem. (*Note:* Practice this when you're procrastinating on a project that some part of you *doesn't want to* do. Remember, your higher, executive brain operates from *choice*— a third place that is neither "you have to" or "I don't want to.")

4. Consider expressing gratitude for this challenge that takes you beyond your usual perspective and puts you in touch with resources and support you didn't know you had. (*Note:* Practice gratitude for a quiet, focused moment when you're paying the bills, facing a writing block, or washing the dishes. Especially, be grateful for how your larger, integrated brain can calmly and creatively work with all aspects of life—even those aspects that you initially resist.)

Mental Toughness: The Focusing Techniques of Peak Performers

When a true champion in any field is losing the event, you can never count him or her out of the game. A champion keeps playing, keeps focused in the moment on a fierce commitment to the mission.

Research on what distracts athletes from an optimal performance has found that thoughts about the future, the outcome, winning, or losing are the biggest obstacles to staying focused. It takes mental toughness to rapidly shift—in one to five seconds—from self-doubts, giving up, wishing it were over, and just wanting the goal, to what you can do now. When you perform optimally—almost effortlessly producing two to four times as much—there's no time to finish cursing; you're a champion, a black-belt martial artist, an expert. You refocus so quickly on the task that they can't see you make the correction. In the Conclusion you will see a chart that will help you link your usual reactions to the corrective actions that are aligned with your mission and vision.

With your mission set as a clear, compelling, magnetic path before you, self-doubt and distractions have less power to gain and hold your attention. Your growing ability to focus on your mission will reduce setbacks and quickly return you to the corrective actions that make success inevitable.

7

Ignite Your Motivation

What motivates you to pursue a distant goal and to keep at it even when difficulties and distractions arise? Is it money, fame, recognition, making a contribution, or the drive to escape the struggles of the past and avoid anticipated pain in the future?

Regardless of whatever external reward motivates you, you know you have an internal motivation to succeed if you've worked hard to complete technical training, a college degree, or a professional license. You know that you must be naturally motivated if you had to put aside immediate gratification to work toward achieving a long-term goal. This is you at your best, acting in accord with your human talents and higher nature.

In spite of evidence to the contrary, all humans are naturally motivated to learn, advance themselves and their families, do good work, and make a contribution to their community. When a person is not exhibiting these human qualities, some fear or negative experience is suppressing this powerful and natural drive to learn and improve. And sometimes it doesn't take much to suppress our energy and keep us stuck in inertia and fear of criticism. Often what is blocking our progress can be like a pebble under the tire of an 18-wheeler that is keeping it from moving forward. Small emotional and cognitive blocks can keep us from seeing new opportunities and creative solutions that ignite our native motivation to break through inertia and get rolling again.

When you are effective and achieve your goals, your human brain produces serotonin and dopamine to give you a burst of pleasure that says "You're on the right path!" When these hormones are depleted through stress and lack of sleep, you feel depressed and lack motivation. In other words, your brain is geared to encourage success with pleasurable feelings and to lower these hormonal pats on the back when you fail or experience pain.

The fact is that—left on its own to run your life—your mammal or animal brain would simply seek pleasure and avoid pain. If you reacted only to your lower brain functions, you would try to avoid pain by procrastinating, feeling anxious, and developing phobias.

But the desire to avoid pain can motivate you to start making changes in your life now.

Three of the greatest motivators are avoidance of pain, positive expectancy, and ownership. You can use the motivating power of future pain—as Dickens did so well with his image of the Ghost of Christmas Future—to face fears, resolve indecision, and take steps today toward a process of change and improvement. Here's an exercise that will demonstrate the power of images of future pain that can help get you unstuck from the comfort of inaction.

Three Great Motivators: Pain, Expectancy, Ownership

Avoidance of Pain: The Ghost of Christmas Future

Exercise: Your Five-year Plan, part 1

Five years have passed. Say to yourself: "The year is X and I am X years old. In the past five years, nothing has changed except that I'm older and heavier. I'm still hoping to achieve the same goals, living in the same place, and facing the same problems."

1. How do you feel, seeing your life without any changes over the course of five years?

2. What absolutely must change? Write down what must change and soon, in 3, 6, or 12 months.

3. Which goals are you still hoping to achieve, with little or no progress over the last five years?

Action Step: What small action step will you take in the next 5 to 30 minutes that will begin to change your life over the next five years?

Exercise: Your Five-year Plan, part 2

Five years have passed. Say to yourself: "The year is X and I am X years old. In the past five years, I have made some marvelous, positive changes. I could not have imagined five years ago that life could be so fulfilling and that I could feel so good about myself and my life. I achieved most of the important goals that I had set for myself back then and resolved old problems. My life, my health, and my relationships are almost ideal."

1. How do you feel, seeing your life with so many positive changes?

2. What are the most important changes in this image of an ideal future?

3. Consider how you started five years ago and what initial steps you took that led to major, transformative changes in how you think of yourself, how you act, and the leadership role you've been playing in managing your life.

4. Say, "It's year X, and five years ago I started to make major changes in my perspective, my sense of who I am, and in my life. Tonight, I will have a party to celebrate with my friends and tell them about my journey."

See yourself in your ideal home, your ideal job, celebrating with new and old friends.

Looking back from five years in the future, consider the big and the small fears and obstacles you've overcome, what you learned, and the changes you've made to reach this ideal level of physical health, financial success and security, and happiness in your relationships.

Write down what you tell your friends about your journey over the last five years:

_____

_____

_____

Action Step: What small action step will you take in the next 5 to 30 minutes that will continue these positive changes in your life over the next five years?

The Power of Positive Expectancy

Nothing has been invented thus far that surpasses the motivating power of a parent's look of expectancy when a child takes his or her first steps. That look carries the child through the risks and pains of failure, through recovery from the tears that come with falling, and through the courage to once again find the motivation to stand on one's own two feet.

We all long for that look that sees the best in us, forgives our failures, and encourages us to once again find the part of us that is strong, robust, joyful, and creative. Employees who have known failure in school and other areas of life long for that look in the eyes of a supervisor, manager, or mentor—a look that will remind them that they have something of value to give, that their potential for excellence is just below the surface. Nothing is quite as powerful as positive expectancy, whether it comes from a parent, a boss, a teacher, or from you.

Use the power of positive expectancy to turn on your brain to persistently and passionately pursue your goals. Knowing that there's a surprise waiting for you gives your mind a blueprint and a road map that alerts you to the right people, the right timing, and the right action steps.

Example: You Will Make a Big Sale Today, Guaranteed

At his California insurance office, Joe was the leading salesperson and leading sales manager for decades. He learned how to inspire and motivate himself when times were tough and figured out how to teach his own strategies to his sales team.

One morning Joe arrived at his new, 18-story office building a few minutes early to prepare for his weekly motivational meeting with his salespeople. In the elevator, he began talking to a man who was unusually happy to meet an insurance salesman. Not only that, the man wanted to buy a $5 million policy! The very surprised Joe said, "Yes, of course, I'll sell you a policy. I'll write it up as soon as I get to my office." Once there, however, Joe realized he could use this rare opportunity to really motivate his sales team.

Joe started his meeting by going through some preliminary information and sales strategies and then told his salespeople: "There is someone in this building who will buy a $5 million policy today!" In seconds, the room cleared out, and 12 salespeople scoured all 18 floors of that building looking for that big sale. Within a few hours, each salesperson had sold one or more policies—some for $1 million, some for $500,000, and one for $5 million.

The expectation that they could earn a large commission that day in that building made each salesperson a success and established an unbroken record of one-day sales, not to mention one-day sales in one building. Each of them faced rejection and failed to sell policies to most of the people they talked to, but they continued to pursue what they knew and believed to be out there.

Knowing a surprise is out there ignites something in your mind, attitude, and appearance that alerts you to the clues to success. It could happen, as it did for Joe, when you give your elevator speech about what you do, or it could result from your conversation with the person seated next to you on the plane. You never know. So expect a surprise. Exercise your own power of positive expectancy.

What positive expectation will you give your brain about what you can achieve today, this week, and this year?

Ownership

Anybody who's ever rented a car or a home knows how very different it feels when you own that car or home and how motivated you are to take care of it. The same applies to your work. If you're working for someone else, you do your job and are motivated by the pay, the support of your coworkers, and—if you're lucky—your interest in the work and the contribution it makes to your community. But when you're working for yourself, you're the boss and you put your heart and soul into a business that is an expression of your creativity and sweat. Now it's easy to put in the extra time and energy it takes to do your best and succeed. Motivation and inspiration are natural and flow easily when you own the business.

Even if you're currently working for someone else, you might feel a sense of ownership toward your projects. If your boss said, "You're not making much progress on this job, and I'm giving it to someone else." You might resent it and even argue, "This is *my* project. I've worked hard to put this together. Now let me see it through to completion."

Your sense of ownership toward your job, your business, and your projects is an important component of feeling motivated to fight for an opportunity to show what you can deliver and put your personal stamp on your work. To ignite your motivation take ownership of your life, your work, your body, your career, and your goals. Avoid the illusion that others—your partner, your parents, your teacher, your boss, or your doctor—can control, own, or take responsibility for your life and work.

If you don't feel a sense of ownership, what can you do today to fully choose and take responsibility for your projects? If you owned, or acted as if you owned, the company:

- How motivated would you be to make it a success?

  _____

  _____

- How motivated would you be to make another call?

  _____

  _____

- What would you do to improve quality, employee satisfaction, and production?

  _____

  _____

- What would you do to reward employee initiative and create incentives for greater efficiency and quality of products and services?

  _____

  _____

- What training would make you more productive, accurate, and efficient?

  _____

  _____

- How would you increase business and reduce costs?

  _____

  _____

Lack of Motivation

If you believe that you lack motivation, use the three key motivators—pain, expectancy, and ownership—to ignite your natural drive. Notice which activities you willingly invest a major portion of time, effort, and money to engage in. Notice how motivated you are to pack up all the equipment, drive for hours, and spend loads of money to play golf, go skiing, scuba dive, or travel to foreign lands. You lack motivation only for activities that you define as boring, perform for a boss, and that make you feel frustrated because of a low probability of recognition and success.

I know high school students who are highly motivated to learn all the words to the latest song and to play music and sports but who seem to lack motivation for algebra, chemistry, or English. I know other students who are studying biochemistry rather than hanging out with their friends because in 10 or 15 years they fully believe they will be doctors or scientists. Where does a teenager find the motivation to study difficult subjects while missing out on having fun with their friends for a goal that is so far in the future and has less than a 50 percent chance of being achieved? You can ask the same question about people who dream of becoming a professional athlete, a movie star, a salesperson, an entrepreneur, or a writer. What causes that level of motivation and persistence?

One possible answer is that it's natural to all human beings, and it simply needs to be focused and encouraged. Another possible answer is that the ability to achieve distant goals is built on the very early ability to stay focused on a future reward and delay gratification for at least 15 minutes. That sounds weird, but, like many counterintuitive concepts, it happens to be true. Let's look at some very interesting and simple research called the marshmallow study.

In *Emotional Intelligence*, Daniel Goleman cites the famous marshmallow study conducted at Stanford with four-year-old day care children who researchers followed up with for 24 years. Each child was given one marshmallow and told that if they could wait, they'd receive a second marshmallow when the researcher returned. When the four-year-olds who could wait 15 minutes to earn a second marshmallow were in high school they scored 210 points higher on their combined SAT scores than their classmates who were unable to delay gratification. The researchers found that a majority of the children who couldn't wait and had eaten their marshmallow had difficulty in school (many not graduating from high school or college), in making friends, and in staying out of trouble with the authorities.

When I'm about to procrastinate on some difficult task, I often think of those four-year-olds sitting relatively still for 15 minutes, waiting for a reward. You may want to tell yourself, as I do, "If a four-year-old can wait 15 minutes, so can I." The fact is, most of us give in to our negative habits, defaults, or favorites within 15 *seconds*. We're grabbing that first marshmallow—checking e-mail or Facebook, texting friends, surfing the Net—when we feel bored, overwhelmed, or stressed. To maintain forward movement on a top-priority project, we just need to get through the first 15 seconds without giving in to that immediate gratification marshmallow. Even a four-year-old can do that.

Tricks to Get Yourself Motivated

1. Make a contract with a friend that you will clean his or her apartment for three hours if you fail to complete an assignment by a specific date. People have been known to put in 60 to 80 hours of work in one month on a project in order to avoid cleaning a friend's place for three hours.

2. Use your full brain to skim books and materials. Look for the essential 20 percent that yields 80 percent of the content—applying the Pareto principle or 80-20 rule. Before you start reading dense material become pro-active in searching for what's the most important. Look for diagrams, lists, questions at the end, and skim opening and closing paragraphs. Begin to read only after your brain is actively involved in seeking answers to the questions you've stirred up by looking at those graphs and lists, and read only relevant paragraphs. See how much of the essential material you can learn in 30 minutes. If you need more time, try another 30 minutes.

3. Put a price on your time, for example, $100 an hour. Estimate how much money you'd be making per hour once you complete your degree or project and how much you'd be losing by delaying the achievement of your goal. This principle works with contractors who are fined thousands of dollars for each day beyond their agreed upon deadline. Each hour of homework could save you $100 or gets you that much closer to earning $100 an hour.

4. Think: "What can I do for myself today for 15 to 30 minutes that will make it easier for me tomorrow?" Make some quick notes, arrange some files, or find the books and telephone numbers you'll need, but get started so tomorrow you can hit the ground running. You'll have already broken through the inertia and begun to feel the momentum. When you show up tomorrow you'll feel as if you have an assistant who makes your life easier and more efficient.

Don't wait for your ego or old self to feel motivated. Getting started is an executive choice; a commitment to your goals and your future. You are naturally motivated to problem solve, learn, and to expect a surprise. Remove a few small pebbles, break through the inertia, and you'll feel the motivation.

8

Effective Goal Setting

The precondition for any human effort is a vision of success. Man is never so strong, so enterprising, so endlessly resourceful, as when his aim stands clearly in front of him, to be achieved by a definite number of determined strides.

—Colin Wilson

Having a goal is easy; after all, it's what you want. But wanting the goal is only the first step. Translating a goal into action steps that lead to success takes more effort than just wanting the goal. Achieving your goals will take drive, passion, persistence, awareness of your weaknesses, and a backup plan when things don't work out on your schedule.

Let's look at why typical goal setting fails and what it takes to set goals that have a greater chance of being effective.

Typical goal setting is dangerous because it creates:

- Anxiety when you try to reach a goal that's in the future—an imaginary place that your body cannot get to—leaving you with energy that's stuck and can't be used now

- Depression when you compare yourself with where you think you *should* be—another imaginary place you can't get to—and conclude that where you are and who you are is bad, or at least inferior to the imaginary place and person you *should* be

- Low self-esteem when you procrastinate, fail, and feel guilty about not progressing toward your goal

- Feelings of being overwhelmed with too many goals and to do lists that you attempt to tackle all at once

- Rigid schedules that will conflict with the reality of life's schedule and, therefore, guaranteeing that something will go wrong because life's not on *your* schedule

- Frustration as you struggle against the reality of where you are and insist on trying to get your body into the imaginary, virtual reality of a future place you think you should be

- Useless wishing for a magical leap into the future where tasks are *done, accomplished, achieved, and complete*, keeping you from taking the necessary, small, repeated action steps on the often rugged path to success

Typical Goal Setting Creates Unrealistic Goals

Let's assume that your goal is to be at work on time at 9 AM. Your idealistic goal is to be up by 6 AM, out the door by 6:15 for a hike or jog of two to three miles, and to see the sun rise over the trees before arriving at work just before 9 AM. Oh, how virtuous you'd feel. Achieving this would be like living in a Disney cartoon with animated birds twittering and adorable bunnies hopping across Technicolor fields. But is it realistic for you and your life now? Or is it likely to lead to repeated failure, frustration, and low self-esteem?

Setting Realistic Goals

The reality is that if you roll out of bed by 8 AM on a work day, you're ahead of the game. And it's a miracle if you get out of the house before 8:45, arriving at work only 15 minutes late for the 9 AM Monday meeting—if there are no traffic jams.

To be realistic, and more effective, your realistic goal would be to get up by 7:30 AM, get dressed, have breakfast, and be out the door by 8:30, arriving at work by 8:55. Your more realistic, achievable goal starts close to where you are now. That way, you're more likely to be successful, and you'll receive a reward from your brain—"Good boy! Good girl! Thank you!"—and increase the frequency of all healthy actions in the right direction.

You still have your idealistic goal, but rather than failing to achieve it, feeling discouraged, and giving up, you're making progress in the right direction. You're encouraging yourself rather than punishing yourself with criticism.

By acknowledging all steps taken by your internal workers that are aligned with your ultimate goal, you're becoming a more effective manager. Once you've achieved the goal of awakening at 7:30, the next step is to see what it takes—how many adjustments you must make—for you to be in bed by midnight so you can set the alarm for 7 AM and get closer to your goal. You'll now have time for some form of exercise without trying to be too idealistic. You may even discover that getting up at 7 AM is a more consistently achievable goal, and you can be grateful that your idealistic goal got you started on the path to a healthy routine and an on-time arrival at work. Doing what it takes is a commitment to persist at getting closer to your goals, no matter how many setbacks. As the Japanese saying goes, "Fall down seven times, get up eight."

What It Takes to Change a Habit and Achieve Your Goals

If you know that you must change a habit—stop smoking, learn a new computer program for your job, or start on projects weeks before the deadline—you also know that you need more than willpower to create the necessary change. One of my goals is to be in bed by 10 PM so I can be up by 6 AM, start on my current writing project for at least 30 minutes, do some exercise, eat a healthy breakfast, and be out the door by 8:45, so I can arrive at my office by 9 AM.

Getting to bed by 10 PM, however, is a goal I repeatedly have failed to achieve. Most evenings, I find myself having the irresistible urge to unwind by watching TV after completing some work. I've experimented with many types of goal setting and have learned what works and what doesn't work for me.

What Doesn't Work

- Willpower or discipline alone
- Education or knowing intellectually that I should or want to change
- Pressure and fear
- Wishing and hoping without follow-through and action steps
- To do lists

What Works

What works in most cases is not discipline—that is, one part of you trying to control another part—or willpower, but rather a structure or behavioral cost. A behavioral cost puts a few extra steps between your initial or default reaction and the habit you want to change. I've learned that if I shut off the TV and take the batteries out of the remote control by 9 PM, I have enough time to do some writing for one of my books, wash up, read, and get ready for bed by 10. When the overwhelming urge to just relax for a few minutes by watching TV occurs, I'm safe about 50 percent of the time. The other 50 percent, I find the batteries and wind up searching for something entertaining and getting to bed at midnight instead of at 10 PM. I've learned that taking the batteries out of the remote control is not a strong enough deterrent for me to change an ingrained habit.

To ensure 100 percent control over my habits, I also need to unplug the TV. Even if I relapse and hunt down the batteries for the remote, I now discover that the TV was unplugged by a wiser, more realistic me. Needing this additional structure to maintain my commitment to a healthy habit is humbling but necessary and effective. I now am enjoying getting to bed by 10 PM and having a full night's sleep while maintaining some control over my lower brain's tendency to do what it wants to do without concern about the consequences I will have to pay in the morning.

Hot Tip

Jump-start your progress on major, overwhelming, top-priority projects with five minutes of brainstorming with a friend over coffee, into a recording device, or in writing. Conduct this session without criticism or censoring; just let it rip. The faster, the better, so your inner critic can't catch up. You'll be amazed at the breakthroughs. Then write down what you can do today and when to start the process.

What's Keeping You Stuck?

It never ceases to amaze me how little it takes to keep some people stuck in the wishing stage of goal achievement without getting to the first small action step. While the blocks often seem to be physical or financial impediments, most are emotional inner conflicts or fears that could be resolved in minutes.

One of my coaching clients is a very successful but overworked entrepreneur who's losing hours each day commuting between three offices of his business. Commuting is costing him business, sleep, and the opportunity to work on his passion for music. Phil has been stuck for more than two years in a common dilemma for entrepreneurs, one of being successful and growing too fast for his resources.

His Goals

1. Limit commuting between three offices to once or twice a week

2. Have more time for his family and fitness

3. Find someone to buy or take over the management of at least one office

4. Build one of his offices to its full potential and sell it within five years

5. Become more proficient at playing the piano and writing music

Phil is dedicated to his customers and finds it difficult to sell his most distant office—more than an hour's commute each way—until he has hired competent staff and increased its profits. The cost of hiring someone to manage the office was prohibitive, as was the cost of hiring a headhunter.

What Worked

I led Phil through the first phase of the five-year Ghost of Christmas Future exercise from the last chapter. He imagined how he would feel if the only things that changed in five years were that commuting cost him one or two car accidents, increases in his car insurance, and tickets for speeding. His children would be older without the benefit of time with their father, and his dream of playing the piano would still be on hold.

Suffering through traffic for five more years was intolerable to Phil. Within a few minutes, he realized that he couldn't live this way for one more year, much less five years. He suddenly felt motivated to take the first steps that were necessary to survive financially and physically.

But we still had to break through the blocks that were keeping him from clearly seeing the issues he could improve. I suggested that we put all his areas of conflict on the back burner for a few minutes and take another look at his goals rather than focusing on his problems. I asked:

- Who can you call in the next hour who could get you an assistant, an intern, or someone to mentor in your business?
- What temp agency supplies part-time people in your business?
- How long would it take to leverage your talent by training two or three interns in your home office?

- If you had competent staff in place in the next year to take care of your favorite customers, could you sell or turn over part of that office?
- What would you have to let go of to reduce your time in your most distant office?
- How long will it take to access the first telephone number or e-mail address?

Notice that these questions shift Phil's focus to what he can *start doing now*. Most were small steps rather than overwhelming changes that would cost him tens of thousands of dollars and massive emotional conflict. The big, future goals were brought into the present, where they could be tackled in small, doable steps.

Phil's eyes lit up as his brain turned on with solutions, ideas, and motivation. Within minutes, Phil was unstuck and excited about the possibility of having more help in his two distant offices, without having to sell them before he was ready.

I said: Phil, you could have figured this out for yourself. You were so busy putting in more time commuting and trying to achieve your ideal goal that you weren't seeing what you can start now. You created several inner conflicts that were keeping you stuck.

You thought that you had to find a buyer for the business and lose the untapped profits that will be coming in over the next few years. You worried about having to come up with the money to pay both a headhunter and an expensive manager while losing contact with the customers you've known for years.

No wonder he couldn't get started. Sometimes the attempted solution is the problem.

The Result

Within an hour of our session, Phil had a lead on three possible candidates who could start as trainees with a possible option of taking over the office within three years. In the meanwhile, Phil could cut back on his time in his most distant office and give greater responsibility to his most experienced employee. Within a few months, he felt he could reduce his office hours and still provide excellent service to his most loyal customers. In a year, Phil will have a better idea of when he can sell one of his offices. He also knows that he'll be getting smarter each day about managing his business rather than having to know everything at once and forcing himself to feel financially and emotionally ready to sell his business.

Hot Tip

You don't have to stay stuck trying to know everything at once before you begin. You don't have to know how to climb the entire mountain. With each step, you'll get smarter and have a better view from which to make a wiser decision about your next step and path. Trying to decide everything from the bottom of the mountain (the start of a major project) is like assuming you'll be dumber tomorrow than you are today. In fact, you're getting smarter with each step once you start.

Taking Action Now!

What small step—a telephone call, an Internet search, a talk with a key employee—could break you free from being stuck and get you moving toward your goal?

Effective Goal Setting: Moving from Want to Action

Effective goal setting has at least four parts.

1. **Setting** the *Ultimate Goal*—a future place you'd like to be and how you'd like to feel in the future. *I want this goal.* For example, become vice president of my company in three years. As vice president, I feel fulfilled and confident that I can do the job and lead the company forward.

2. **Choosing** the *Path* that leads toward that goal. I *am willing to do the work to get to my goals. I choose this path.* For example, I'm willing to work for three years to learn new skills, make contacts, follow up with customers, and make the necessary habit changes that will position me to take on the responsibilities of vice president.

3. **Committing** to each step along the path with a *Functional Goal* that tells you where to start and what to do on the path to your ultimate goal. I *am committed to traveling the entire path, regardless of obstacles or setbacks.* For example, I will start today by making three extra follow-up calls to clients, signing up for a class

about selling on the Internet, and putting the TV remote control in the garage.

4. **Starting Now!** *When can I start? On what part of the task will I start?* For example, I will start for 5, 15, or 30 minutes by writing out my thoughts, searching for specific information and contacts, calling or e-mailing someone for advice, or just brainstorming a blueprint, flowchart, or outline of what I can do over the next few weeks or six months.

Bottom Line

Effective goal setting requires a process that goes beyond just wanting the ultimate goal. If you have only an ultimate goal, you will remain overwhelmed by the amount of work involved in moving from where you are to where you want to be. To be consistently effective in setting and achieving your goals, you'll need a clear path, a commitment to each step along that path, and a functional goal that tells you when and where to start, and what to do today on the path to achieving your goals.

Wish Upon a Star

One evening at dinner, just before I was to give a presentation at Rancho La Puerta on effective goal setting, four-year-old Sarah asked me what I was going to talk about. I told Sarah that I was going to give a speech about how to make dreams come true. When she brightened and said, "I know how to do that," I encouraged her to tell me how. With a shrug, Sarah said, "You find the first star, tell it your wish, and then go to sleep. And when you wake up, your dream comes true."

Later that evening, Sarah sat in the front row with her mother, eager to tell my audience how to set effective goals. After she charmed the audience with her version of how to make dreams come true, I told them that Sarah had included an element that I had forgotten: You, the conscious you, must go to sleep. That is, setting a goal is not a process of constant, conscious-mind struggle. There's a magic to it that includes your dreaming mind and your subconscious genius working on pulling together information and resources from inside you and from your surroundings. One day soon, you'll feel a tap on the shoulder that awakens you to the fact that the process has been unfolding once you've set it in motion.

Effective Goal-Setting Quiz

Answer yes or no to the following questions.

1. Do I have *in writing* a clearly defined set of lifetime goals, five-year goals, one-year goals, and six-month goals?

2. Do I know when I will start today on a lifetime goal? On a top-priority short-term goal?

3. Do I start on the top-priority task early in my day?

4. Do I set priorities according to the importance of the activity, not its urgency?

5. Do I delegate tasks that are not in my area of strength or expertise?

6. Do I have a system for preventing unnecessary intrusions of mail and calls from reaching my desk?

7. Do I have a system for filing that follows the principle: Do it, delegate it, or dump it?

8. Do I have a system for keeping my home and leisure time a haven and sanctuary from the work of the office?

9. Do I make minor decisions quickly, considering the value of my time?

10. Do I summarize the issues and decisions made at meetings, ensuring that responsibilities are clearly assigned for action and follow-through?

More than three no answers indicates where you have difficulties with goals, priorities, and time management. Review these questions periodically to ensure that you are spending your time and energy on the activities essential for taking the steps that will achieve your top priorities and lead to success.

9

Managing Procrastinators and Difficult Employees

If you've ever tried to herd cats, get teenagers to clean their room, or get a timely response from a procrastinator, you know that your usual management instincts are useless. Yet, all of us—procrastinators, producers, and workaholics—must work with, live with, and relate to individuals whose problems with procrastination cause us delays, frustration, and missed deadlines.

Putting pressure on procrastinators only backfires. You need a strategic plan—for dealing with them *and* with yourself. Without a strategy, your usual approach will unwittingly encourage and contribute to the procrastination patterns of those you manage and supervise.

Hot Tip

Strategic psychology tells us that "the attempted solution maintains the problem." The so-called cause of the problem is in the past, but your behavior today and what you're telling yourself about the problem keep the symptoms alive. Notice how your way of trying to solve a problem is keeping you enmeshed in something that started years ago. Let go of trying so hard in the wrong direction—pushing on the pull door—and you may find that you're able to sidestep the big problems the way a matador steps aside from a charging bull, refusing to butt heads with a larger piece of reality.

Procrastinators Use Ineffective Self-Talk

Employers, managers, and parents will be more effective in managing procrastinators when they understand the counter-productive self-talk procrastinators use with themselves and resist the temptation to contribute to it.

Procrastinators tend to pressure themselves with "I have to finish something big, do it perfectly, and endure self-criticism and endless periods of deprivation and pain."

This is in sharp contrast to the effective producers who manage themselves by saying, "I choose to start for 15 minutes on one small step and do a rough draft so I can enjoy my leisure time guilt-free." For producers, focused work is a sanctuary free of interruptions—almost like a vacation from worry about other demands. For procrastinators, work is like being in solitary confinement in prison with a critic.

To effectively manage people who procrastinate, steer them away from the usual negative self-management language of procrastinators and toward that of effective producers. Keep in mind that four main issues are at the heart of most procrastination problems:

1. Feeling afraid of failure—as a result of equating their self-worth with their work

2. Feeling like a victim—as a result of pressuring themselves with "you have to" statements that lead to resentment, resistance, and rebellion from a part that reacts with "I don't want to"

3. Feeling overwhelmed—as a result telling themselves "You have to finish an enormous task" at some vague point in the imagined future and tackle all parts at once

4. Feeling a need to be perfect—as a result of low self-worth and the need to avoid criticism

These four problem areas point to four possible solutions:

1. Task-focus versus defending against criticism

Employees who feel that they must constantly consider "Is the boss going to be angry at me again? Will I be good enough? Will I be fired if I fail?" have their capacity for productive work compromised by worrying about keeping their job and defending their self-worth. To help employees achieve maximum long-term efficiency, offer them the personal safety and respect that allows them to focus on doing their job rather than on fear that they'll be judged, criticized, and possibly fired.

Although an employee's personal insecurity is not the manager's problem, she can create a safe environment in which it's possible to focus on the task of improving the product or service rather than worrying about being shamed or demeaned for mistakes.

2. Choice versus compliance

Telling someone he "has to" or "should" do something implies a threat from an outside authority that is forcing a victim to do something against his will. These messages almost always evoke resistance and resentment that are expressed through procrastination, non-compliance, and other passive-aggressive behaviors such as coming in late and sabotage.

To drastically reduce procrastination, offer options to employees that stimulate creativity and motivation, rather than making demands and threats. When they are given clear options, properly motivated employees have been known to willingly choose to face challenges that require cooperation and hard work.

Consider how doctors and nurses worry about patient *compliance* with hospital rules, when most patients have repeatedly indicated that they would be eager to participate in their health care if given the opportunity to make *choices* about their food, sleep, and medical decisions. Give people choices rather than demanding compliance, and you will ignite their natural motivation to actively participate in enhancing their health and their work performance.

3. Focus on starting versus finishing

Focusing on the finish line makes it difficult to get off to a good start. Overwhelmed by the importance of a task and the immensity of the work involved, the procrastinator will try to do it all at once—creating anxiety or panic—and then will avoid the task in an attempt to reduce his discomfort.

Ineffective Managers say, "You have to finish this project." While this statement has the advantage of being direct, it shows a lack of understanding of the procrastinator's problems with realistic time limits, setting priorities, and a tendency to feel overwhelmed. It also leaves the procrastinator focused on the finishing point in the imaginary future, without any indication that there's an agreed-upon starting point and a need for periodic progress reports.

Effective Managers say, "When can you start on a rough, rough draft?" The answer to this question will let you know if you have properly communicated your sense of urgency about the project and the level of quality that is needed for your first review.

Ask the employee, "When will you *start?*" A true procrastinator will give you a vague answer, such as "next week" or "tomorrow." The number of times you must ask the question is a barometer of the depth of the person's procrastination and lack of a realistic image of time. It may take four questions before the employee mentally checks his schedule and gives his brain a clear image of when to start today, such as "at 2:15."

Understand that you're not trying to micromanage; you're helping the employee speak to himself in a language that directs his mind and body to the work station to start on the project at a specific time. By using this simple structure, he will learn to become a more effective self-manager of his time and projects.

Effective managers understand the importance of communicating to their employees—and themselves— the specific action steps required to *begin* the task. They also understand that overcoming start-up inertia is half the battle. To work optimally, a clear picture is needed of the time, the place, the task, and of the ability to "choose to start."

That is, you can turn a procrastinator into a producer by teaching him to ask himself, "When can I start, on what, and where?"

4. Perfectionism versus self-acceptance

Criticizing employees will lead some to try to be perfect in a futile attempt to avoid mistakes. It serves as a defense against having their worth and work judged. Being perfect is, of course, impossible, but the attempt is a terrible waste of time and causes delays in the completion of many projects. If you can, help the perfectionistic employee to accept himself or herself as perfectly human.

To ensure that an employee doesn't waste time trying to be perfect, say, "Get back to me in three hours so I can give you feedback on what to do next." This method of frequent feedback sessions will also help you clarify your own thoughts about the direction of the project and give you a more accurate estimate of how much time it will take the employee to complete a good-enough draft. Receiving frequent feedback has been found to help employees monitor their behavior and ensure that they are aligned with your goals and deadlines.

As you begin to communicate to employees that you respect their worth and dignity as a person, they will eliminate much of their defensive, fearful thinking and behaviors that are the chief causes of procrastination. They will learn to focus more quickly on optimal job performance rather than the need to be perfect in an attempt to avoid anticipated criticism.

Hot Tip

Advanced time management and habit change skills require that in addition to asking yourself when, where, and on what you will work, you also ask yourself, "Even if X happens?" As in: "I'm committed to starting at 2:15 even if I start late or am distracted

by hunger, anxiety, e-mail, or a loss of confidence."
Write down some of your favorite even-if statements
and link them to corrective action in order to build
neural circuits in your brain that make it easier to
maintain healthy, productive habits.

A Manager's Challenge:
The Difficult Employee

I grew up in Jersey City, New Jersey, when gangs ran the streets
and intimidated schoolkids for their lunch money. Before I
reached 15, I had my nose broken twice fighting back against
these bullies. Starting in high school, I worked 15 to 20 hours a
week to help out my family, while most of my classmates were
free to hang out and have fun. So I grew up with a chip on my
shoulder, and I remained irreverent and distrustful of authority
for many years into my adulthood. On some of my early jobs, *I*
was the difficult, disrespectful employee who talked back to
supervisors and even my captains in the Army.

When I was in graduate school, I was hired to administer
intelligence tests to some very difficult subjects, prison inmates.
When there was group testing in the main hall, the ringleaders
stood out because they were the loudest and most difficult to
manage. It was these same men who, in the one-on-one testing
sessions, tearfully pleaded that I teach them how to read. They
had to act tough in front of the other prisoners but, because they
couldn't read or sit still in grammar school, carried chips on
their shoulders and a sense of shame and low self-esteem since
childhood. The same is true of many difficult employees.

It's possible that their challenges to authority were attempts to hide their sense of inadequacy and that their childhood failures in school led them toward crime in an effort to gain some recognition for their abilities and a feeling of success.

These days, when I work with a former gang member like Will (not his real name), who's been in trouble with the law and has had difficulties keeping a job, I see the bully in him and yet understand his shame, frustration, and rage. So I considered it a supreme compliment when Will told me how much our work helped him change from his former explosive rage to a state of inner peace and calm power. He's much less likely to use his physical power to try to control a situation and is able to focus his mind on finishing the apprenticeship requirements for his job. He has gone from being reactive and ready to fight to being, in his words, like a Nelson Mandela, a Gandhi, and a Dalai Lama.

Will has learned to use some of the exercises I've offered you in this book, such as pausing for a few breaths when under pressure and focusing his mind on his higher objectives rather than on the perceived injuries to his pride. He's become an outstanding employee who—while remaining very direct in his straight-from-the-shoulder way of communicating—uses his mind and his words rather than fists and weapons to express his side of an argument. His energy has been turned toward making something positive happen in his community, his family, and his job. Now that Will has a meaningful outlet for his talents and drive, he can display the qualities of an entrepreneur and a leader that previously were hidden. In a sense, all he needed was some alternative, healthier coping skills and an opportunity to express them in a work environment where his worth as a person is acknowledged and respected.

Negative Attention versus Positive Incentives and Recognition for Positive Action

These real-world experiences, combined with psychological and business perspectives allow me to bring a unique synthesis of skills to my seminar participants and CEO, COO, entrepreneurial, and management clients.

When managers tell me of their problems with a difficult employee who can't be fired, I often notice that the difficult employee is receiving a lot of attention for his negative behaviors, but little is said about what he's doing right. In fact, by acting out, he's getting attention that reinforces the problem behaviors, while he and others are not receiving recognition for their positive work that contributes to the organization.

To increase positive behaviors, you must reward all small steps in the right direction, as did students in a college behavioral psychology course. They demonstrated they had learned the material by reinforcing certain behaviors in their professor. Unbeknownst to their professor, they conspired to ignore him by looking down whenever he was on the left side of the classroom and to reinforce his movement to the right side of the room by looking up and smiling. Within just a few classes, the professor was spending more than 90 percent of his time on the right side.

It doesn't take much to give recognition to someone who has had little opportunity to be appreciated and succeed. A smile, a nod of the head to show respect, and a "Yes, that's right" is enough to reward, reinforce, and thus increase desired positive behaviors. Given a chance to prove themselves, even individuals with some of the most tragic histories have been known to become loyal employees who are eager to show that they can make a positive contribution. But you may want to prepare yourself to identify those employees who are especially difficult to manage because of their potential for violence.

Managing the Problem Employee

The best time to prepare for defusing potentially violent people is now. . . . By planting the pathways in your mind of effective responses, you will increase the likelihood that you will avoid violent behavior directed toward you.

—Bruce Blythe, *Blindsided: A Manager's Guide to Catastrophic Incidents in the Workplace*

The CEO of Crisis Management International, Bruce Blythe, offers insights into the minds of employees who could become violent. A former Marine and consultant to the FBI, Blythe believes that a crisis preparedness program and training are essential these days for any company, large or small.

It makes sense for all managers and supervisors to be aware of the signals that one of their employees could be triggered to act violently when provoked. Such employees have a tendency to blame others—especially minorities, immigrants, and supervisors—for their problems and failures. They often have deep feelings of inferiority, insecurity, and inadequacy that they mask and compensate for by boasting, intimidating others, and bullying.

The violence-prone personality tries to avoid feelings of inadequacy by acting superior to others and by trying to manipulate and control others. Yet he feels entitled and self-righteous about seeking vengeance because he's been lowered, put down, or *dissed* (disrespected) and feels he is just fighting to gain the respect he deserves and to eradicate the shame he feels for having been humiliated. Most bullies and abusers have been bullied and abused in childhood and prefer to identity with the aggressor rather than see themselves as the victim.

His frustration and exacting version of fairness serve as a rationale for taking retribution and abusing others. He feels justified and sees his behavior as rational, just the way a driver on the freeway feels justified in acting out his road rage because someone cut him off or refused to get out of his way.

How Can Managers Defuse Violence?

Ideally, you would treat the violence-prone employee with the same respect you treat all employees but with an awareness of their sensitivity to criticism and unfairness. You don't pamper their egos, but you avoid actions that could activate defensive, aggressive, or violent behavior. Most employees will not turn to violence as their first way of coping with tension or perceived unfairness, but some may when provoked. Experts on violence management, such as Blythe, suggest that violence-prone individuals can remain calm when employers manage to dampen the intensity, duration, and frequency of provoking actions.

Keep the intensity and the volume of your speech under control. Limit discussions to the level of active listening rather than arguing and debating. Use your superior communications skills to keep disagreements from becoming shouting matches. Use the employee's name and say, "Yes" or "Yes, and" while avoiding "No" and "No, you have to." Avoid demeaning comments that might threaten the employee's sense of worth and safety. Give employees choices and alternatives that maintain their self-esteem.

Limit the frustration of employees (and customers) by ensuring that they are informed of how long they will have to wait, and give them an alternative time for a callback or a new appointment. When the time spent waiting on the phone or in an office exceeds 15 minutes, it's annoying to most of us, but it can be perceived as an extreme insult by those whose hostility is easily triggered.

Be alert to how often your employees and customers must repeat requests and complaints before your managers answer. Hostility is more likely to be provoked by repeated incidents of supervisory negative comments or failures to listen to complaints than when such events occur rarely.

Use assertiveness techniques in which you start with I-statements rather than accusations and finger pointing. For example: "I have a problem. I want to work with you and give you a chance to show what you can do here. But I'm concerned that my boss is going to tell me I made a mistake in hiring you. It would make it lot easier on both of us if you could show up on time without any arguments with your coworkers. That would allow me to give you a positive evaluation."

That is, avoid pointing fingers with "You have a problem." Since you—as the manager, supervisor, or owner—are the one with the goal and responsibility, you're the one with a problem to solve. Spell out the specific behavioral goals, such as showing up on time and avoiding conflicts with coworkers.

Respect Your Employees and Minimize Difficulties

Like all of us, problem employees want to feel heard and understood and want to be treated with respect. Avoid arguing: Listen and paraphrase their words so employees know you've been listening. Avoid cornering or pressuring any person who appears agitated or panicked.

Use your superior customer service communication skills to hear out complaints and requests and to ask for clarification on how the incident or unfairness might be resolved. By respecting your customers and your employees, you'll defuse violent tendencies and minimize difficulties with potentially problematic individuals.

Brain research shows that our brains learn faster and continue to grow when we have something meaningful to do. If you want fully engaged, efficient, and effective employees, give them meaningful work that makes a difference in the lives of the community and contributes to their own well-being and that of their coworkers. Jim Goodnight, CEO of SAS (Business Analytics Software)—which ranked #1 on *Fortune* magazine's 2010 list of the 100 Best Companies to Work For—says: "Treat employees like they make a difference and they will." People at SAS work hard because they're motivated to take care of a company that takes care of them.

Treat Your Employees Like Customers

After ten years of struggling to become a superior company, we finally came to our senses and figured out that we would never be world class until every person could play a meaningful role in determining how we were going to run the business and improve our operations.

    —Don Wainwright, *CEO of Wainwright Industries, winner of the Malcolm Baldrige National Quality Award*

Year after year, the research and surveys report that satisfied employees produce satisfied customers. Take a look at *Fortune* magazine's yearly list of the 100 Best Companies to Work For—for example, SAS, Google, DreamWorks, W. L. Gore, Edward Jones, Whole Foods, Genentech, and Nordstrom—and you'll find companies that are supportive of their employees and yet incredibly successful financially. These companies emphasize employee training and safety, encourage suggestions and involvement in ongoing improvement and cost reductions, and often provide on-site child care. In a word, these are companies that are employee-focused and yet far surpass their competition in customer satisfaction while lowering product defects, accidents, sick days, and employee turnover. These are companies where the employees say, "This is a great company to work for. I love coming to work."

Training, Support, and Control over Work Improve Employee Satisfaction

Studies of workplace behavior and health have been summarized in the journal *Anxiety, Stress, and Coping:* "High time pressure, low control, and low social support are associated with lower well-being," leading to greater distress, job dissatisfaction, and absenteeism. To create healthier work environments, workers need some control over how they work and the support of their supervisors and coworkers.

Conclusion

- To lower the health care costs of your employees, increase supervisor support.
- To lessen absenteeism, increase the amount of control employees have over their day-to-day work routines.
- To lower distress, illness, and employee dissatisfaction, increase both control and supervisor support.
- To lessen psychological distress, make sure there are clear deadlines with challenges within the employee's ability to handle them.
- To build employee confidence, productivity, and efficiency, increase training.

Training in basic job and interpersonal skills gives employees the self-confidence to take more initiative, make suggestions, and continuously improve the organization.

Employees at The Container Store receive more than 200 hours of training, although the industry average is only 8 hours. One of their highly trained employees equals three of the competition's, says CEO Kip Tindell. By hiring and training the best people, The Container Store has cut costs and built a solid reputation with customers.

Your employees are your internal customers. Their satisfaction is really a measure of how well they are supported by their supervisors and peers and how empowered they are to resolve areas of dissatisfaction for both internal and external customers. Maximize the unique potential of each individual. Help your employees grow and succeed, and you'll foster loyalty, lower turnover, and greater customer satisfaction.

Regardless of the size of your organization or private business you can share in the same success as *Fortune's* 100 Best Companies to Work For if you will treat your employees with the same respect you give your customers. The results will be improved customer satisfaction scores, improved revenues and profits, and significantly lower health care costs and turnover than the competition.

You still may not be able to herd cats, but by practicing these strategies you can become a more effective manager of procrastinators and difficult employees. You may even help them to tap their innate motivation and natural drive to contribute meaningful work to their organization and community.

Conclusion

Applications and Fine-Tuning

You miss 100 percent of the shots you don't take.
—Wayne Gretzky, hockey great

Let's Put the Theory into Practice

We've all heard the saying, "If you continue to repeat the same patterns, you'll continue to get the same results." But you want a different, outstanding result—one that's aligned with your goals, your new sense of what's possible, and the dynamic new skills you're ready to put into practice. The strategies and tactics you've been learning have helped change your mental programming, and you now are ready to design a more fulfilling life for yourself, your family, and your organization.

At this stage in *The Now Habit at Work* process, you've become familiar with your default distractions and habits. By doing the exercises in the earlier chapters, you've gained some distance from the critical "should" inner voice, the "what if" worrier voice, and the part of you that says, "But I don't know how." You now have a new vantage point from which to see and hear these limited aspects of yourself, a vantage point that enables you to play your proper leadership role and maintain control of your life and career.

These changes in perspective and role allow you to quickly shift from using pressure and criticism—which may have caused inner conflict, self-sabotage, and loss of motivation—to more effective leadership methods. In your role as an effective leader, you're empowered to guide all aspects of yourself in protecting your life, your body, and your career from destructive habits, substances, and concepts. Now, you are the one in charge, not your old programs that operated from fear, self-doubt, and stress.

Hot Tip

Use special days such as New Year's, the Solstice, or your birthday to let go of past problems and regrets and to create a new perspective, a new identity, and a new life for the coming year.

You'll still need to confront old fears and habits and the discomfort of changing familiar patterns, but success is inevitable when you start backing up your intentions with daily effort. Now you're ready to replace the all too familiar patterns of the past with the courageous action that will help you achieve a more successful career and a more fulfilling life.

Applying the Tools and Accessing Your New Skills

Now that you have the right knowledge, you are ready to take the right action. You can start applying these tools immediately, but practice them first before testing yourself during a crisis. Start by accessing these tools on a daily basis and they will literally be at your fingertips, in the front of your mind, and an organic part of your newer, more effective self-management repertoire. Within weeks, these new concepts, strategies, and tactics will come to you automatically, and you'll wonder why you didn't use them years ago.

Instead of driving down the freeway looking in the rear-view mirror to check on your past and where you've been, you can look forward to the opportunities that are in your future. Instead of basing current decisions on your former identity and insecurities, you can start tasks today that will benefit your future self, making it easier to see them to completion because you've already broken through the inertia and are onto momentum. Your future self will be grateful that last week, last month, and last year you got things started by taking the initial steps on the road to greater success and health and a stronger sense of self.

Use Old Habits to Switch to More Effective Alternatives

Unless you've prepared a plan, unavoidable stressful events could cause you to fall back into the old habit of reaching for your favorite fix in an attempt to reduce tension. After all, your familiar patterns have been around for a long time, and you've been accessing them as survival mechanisms for decades. It may take a few dozen times of shifting to your newer, more effective habits before you easily access healthy alternatives and completely replace negative habits. Remember that each time you choose a healthy alternative to your former, limited methods of coping, you're strengthening new neural pathways in your brain that lead you in new, positive directions.

To change to more effective, updated behaviors, you'll have to let go of what feels comfortable and natural. Consider that what seems to come naturally in fact may have been learned when you were a child and accepted as natural before you had the ability to decide for yourself. Beginning skiers, for example, are often taught to form a snowplow wedge with their skis and to stop by turning uphill. This works on the bunny slopes but causes loss of control and panic on steeper, more interesting, often icier ski slopes. It also doesn't allow the skier to enjoy the excitement of skiing under control down the intermediate and advanced trails.

Reverting to your snowplow wedge or your favorite habit when faced with a business crisis will not take you where you want to go. And reverting to old habits doesn't allow you to work on the more challenging, lucrative projects that will advance your career.

A skier who wants to gain control of his skis and improve his skills must replace what feels natural with the counter-intuitive technique of looking and turning downhill. The same is true in business: To advance to the more interesting, challenging, and fulfilling jobs, you must get out of your comfort zone—what feels natural—and face the discomfort of learning alternative ways of coping, new computer programs, and new strategic plans.

As an effective manager of yourself—using the language of effective leaders—you would link your current habit to a corrective action. For example, an effective ski instructor wouldn't tell a novice skier to turn his skis downhill while in the snowplow wedge. That's too overwhelming and would only result in greater fear, reliance on the counterproductive snowplow, loss of control, and possible injury. Nor would an effective manager say to an employee, "Take charge of this campaign and try not to screw it up this time."

An effective instructor, coach, or manager would help the student, client, or employee to identify their current tendency—which for the novice skier might be moving his hands and skis in the usual uphill direction. The effective instructor might say, "Now that you're aware of your usual way of trying to stay in control, do the opposite and move your hands over your downhill knee and you'll begin to turn easily. Repeat this movement for each turn, and you'll turn sooner, be in control, and have greater stopping power because your weight will be over your downhill ski."

Use the same principle of linking from your current, counterproductive reactions—such as feeling overwhelmed and procrastinating on calls to customers—to your new, more effective habit of choosing to face uncomfortable tasks immediately. Expect that your former way of coping will come to you first, bringing with it old thoughts, feelings, and cravings. Take at least one to three breaths—that's just 5 to 15 seconds—to give yourself time to choose to activate your new, more effective alternative.

Notice what initially feels natural and comfortable—your default habit—and switch to the new behavior, which initially feels uncomfortable. Practice this switching technique several times in a safe situation and on a safe hill before tackling a project that is the equivalent of trying to ski from the top of the mountain during a blizzard.

Rehearsing for Long-Term Success

Working toward a goal that is essential to your health and career is worthwhile, even if you start later than planned, break your commitment for a day or two, or procrastinate on getting started. Don't let slips, setbacks, mistakes, and disappointments derail your progress. Planning for a long-term commitment requires that you include methods for recovery from normal

Hot Tip

Give yourself 5 to 15 seconds before running away from an overwhelming project. There's a certain inertia that must be broken through when you start any new habit or face a difficult, uncomfortable task or activity. It takes only a few seconds for your brain to search for an alternative solution when you don't accept the favorite it initially offers you. The body takes longer to warm up to the idea of walking or jogging—almost six minutes before the muscle fibers are lubricated and have stopped hurting. If you're going to start an exercise program, you want to get past those first six minutes—about half a mile of walking—to a second wind, when it becomes easier and even pleasurable. Break through the inertia to get to momentum and motivation, and both your brain and your body will help you out.

and understandable lapses. Part of that plan is to cut short any self-criticism so you can minimize the likelihood of going into a tailspin of lost confidence, low motivation, and giving up on your goals.

Another part of your plan might include a mental rehearsal of slipping and rapid recovery. In your mental rehearsal, no one gets hurt, you don't risk getting your boss or customers angry because of your delays, and you won't get fired.

Let's consider a mental rehearsal in which you revert to an old habit of wasting time on the details of a large project to avoid feeling overwhelmed by looking at the big picture. You're procrastinating, but you think of it as perfectionism. In fact, you might feel self-righteous about putting in extra time on the details and doing extra research before actually producing anything. You may find yourself using a number of old escape patterns, such as craving sweets, making more phone calls, trying to make a perfect decision that no one could criticize, or discovering 10 other things that seem urgent and require immediate attention. If you fall into your old pattern once again, make sure you know how to access and use your new alternatives. Now's the time to practice recovering from a setback before you waste any more time staying stuck.

In the past, slipping into old patterns might have generated a lot of self-criticism and lowered your self-esteem, causing you sleepless nights, worries about failing to meet expectations, and a general lack of confidence. But this time, you know how to access your new skills of focusing on the task, creating inner safety, and using more of your brain to creatively problem-solve rather than reverting to negative patterns. You're finally ready to play a leadership role—one that will challenge you to access the skills you've put in place in the past few weeks—and achieve an optimal performance.

Long-Term Success: Build Resilience to Setbacks

If you want to make long-term sustainable progress, it is essential to anticipate setbacks and be prepared with tactics that help you rapidly bounce back. The effort required to achieve consistent progress is not monumental, but it takes planning and preparation to maintain your commitments under pressure, setbacks, and periodic stressors. The process of integrating these tools and expanding your repertoire of skills is unique to you, your career, and your work environment, but nevertheless, it will be a process—one of moving forward and then reverting to old patterns when you're under pressure.

You don't need to be a rocket scientist or a psychic to predict that within the next 60 to 90 days, all of us will experience an event—urgent deadlines, computer crashes, taxes, or the flu—that will make us want to escape to our favorite distraction or addiction. Studies of effective habit-change programs have shown that after 60 days of progress in changing difficult habits such as smoking, increasing exercise, and improving diet, most participants will stop using the basic strategies that initially were so powerful. When the inevitable stressful event occurs, they tend to revert to old, familiar habits. To prevent throwing out weeks of progress because of one or two bad days, you need a plan B to prepare for, and recover from, a setback.

Tightrope walkers, for example, know that they become dependent on the 16-foot balancing pole to keep them from falling. They also know that under certain conditions—such as when a sudden breeze pushes them too far into a fall—holding on to the same pole that saved their lives dozens of times before would contribute to a serious accident. So they practice a plan B, throwing away the pole and grabbing for the wire. In football, a quarterback can't rely just on his passing game. He must practice handing off the ball to his running back and running the ball himself to avoid getting sacked behind the line of scrimmage. If you know that you're overly dependent on one way of coping in business, you'd be wise to develop an alternative and practice accessing it so you can have it handy when under pressure.

> ## Hot Tip
>
> Place red check marks on your calendar or Excel sheet, and number every successful day of maintaining your commitments to your goals—getting to work early, not smoking, abstaining from sugar, avoiding checking your e-mail until you've completed at least 30 minutes of work. Skip over those days when you lapse or slip, and continue counting the next day. If, for example, you revert to an old pattern of surfing the Internet on day 30 as a diversion from a difficult project, skip that day and count the next as your thirtieth day of maintaining your commitment to your mission. Remember that you're keeping a record to motivate yourself to stick with your commitments, not for self-criticism or self-punishment.
>
> Think of lapses as an opportunity to practice rapidly recovering from setbacks, learn more about what it takes to stay on track, and build on the progress you've made toward your goal. You'll want to incorporate what you've learned from your mistakes and stay alert to those situations that make you vulnerable to reverting to outdated ways of coping.

Planning for Recovery from Setbacks: Mental Rehearsal

When you did the exercises in earlier chapters, you were laying down alternative neural tracks in your brain that can direct your train of thought to new destinations instead of dropping you off at the same old stations of anxiety, procrastination, and depression. You now can use your awareness of your former patterns to alert you to switch to a track that is aligned with your current skills, knowledge, and opportunities. Within a few weeks of practice, you will be able to switch more readily and confidently from the old pattern to your new, more effective executive leadership skills.

Luckily, you don't have to completely eliminate your old patterns or relinquish your old identity to establish a new, more effective alternative. In fact, you can use your former familiar patterns to alert you to the opportunity to exercise the new skills and choices you have now.

To put the odds for positive change in your favor, you may want to plan a controlled setback so you can consciously observe the start of your reactive patterns and redirect their energy into corrective action. Each time you consciously refuse to use an old pattern, its control over you weakens, and you gain a few more degrees of freedom to choose an updated, more effective way of coping. Now that you have those healthier alternatives in place, you may want to test them the way a driver might go into a controlled skid on ice to practice letting up on the gas and turning the wheel without hitting the brakes, or the way a pilot practices recovering from the loss of engine power. During practice, you get to learn from your mistakes in a safe environment, and you learn to override emotional and cognitive tendencies that could be costly in a real situation.

Exercise: Rehearse Recovering from a Setback

Whenever I face a project that appears overwhelming or boring, I get this feeling in the pit of my stomach that quickly leads to thoughts about escaping because it's too complicated, too hard, or just a waste of time. I've learned that if I don't catch this pattern within seconds, I will find myself thinking, "Let's get out of here and do something that's easier and more fun." Once I began to observe the very start of these reactions and thoughts, I found that most of the time I can stop this avoidance process before it pulls me into a swamp of wasted time surfing the Net or eating snacks.

As you become familiar with your own microreactions, you'll improve your ability to choose to start and stay with difficult but important projects through the initial inertia so you can get onto momentum, motivation, and creative solutions.

To get a better sense of the microreactions that subconsciously may lead you to seek comfort in destructive, and often fattening, external fixes to an internal state, do this exercise with your eyes closed. Notice, for example, the common feelings of inner conflict, ambivalence, and resentment that often precede procrastination; the criticism that precedes perfectionism; and the fear that precedes stress. Also notice the hurt feelings, frustration, and anger that lead you to say something to a customer, a boss, or coworker that you'll later regret. Do a mental rehearsal of the situations in which you are likely to feel stressed, embarrassed, or resentful so you can observe your reactions, choose how to act, and prepare your brain with an alternative track that leads to the achievement of your higher goals and mission.

Here are some examples of business challenges that my clients face that you might use and apply to your work situation:

- Being assigned responsibility for a large project and the management of teams for your firm's best customer

- Working with or for a construction-architecture firm and coordinating with the city planner, the client, and the subcontractors
- Contacting a disgruntled customer or client after delaying a follow-up response to a complaint
- Having to complete a complex computer programming project that will be delivered to the customer weeks behind schedule

Mental Rehearsal

See yourself in a scene that fits your work situation and current responsibilities. Close your eyes so you can observe more accurately your physical reactions, which emotions arise, and your inner dialogue. Once you've identified your default reactions, write down what you've observed in each category.

- **Physical Reactions:** Notice areas of muscle tension, changes in heart rate, butterflies in your stomach, and other symptoms of a stress response, such as cold, damp hands. Notice if your body posture changes into a depressive or shamed slump or one of angry defiance.
- **Emotional Reactions:** Notice how your feelings change as you see yourself about to take on this project. Pay attention to fear, feeling overwhelmed, anxiety, and any other responses of worry. Notice any fatigue and loss of motivation.
- **Inner Dialogue:** Notice how you talk to yourself. Is your default inner dialogue one of criticism, pressure, and "you have to" or is it supportive and helpful?

Applying the Language of Effective Managers

How you talk to yourself will affect how you feel about any project or task. If you've been procrastinating on an important goal, it's very likely that what you initially told yourself you *want* to achieve has become something you now tell yourself you *have to* or *should* do. The goal you previously associated with a joyful sense of achievement—such as running a marathon or mastering a computer program—now brings feelings of pressure, resistance, and guilt for failing to follow through on your promise to yourself and others. A participant in one of my seminars wrote: "I've been watching how I use 'You should finish working on that account' and am turning it into 'I'm choosing to start.' That really reduces a lot of stress! Also, I've been starting things for a small half-hour, and sometimes, before I know it, two hours have passed."

- What do you say to yourself?
  ["have to" or "choose to"]

  _____

  _____

- What is your attitude?
  [self-blaming or task-oriented]

  _____

  _____

- What is your goal?
  ["just finish" or commit to entire process]

  _____

  _____

- What lowers your anxiety?

  [future-worrying or making a plan now]

  _____

  _____

Link Initial Reactions to Corrective Action

Become aware of the automatic link between your initial thoughts and the reactions they produce. This mental rehearsal will prepare you to rapidly shift to corrective actions that will guide you toward optimal performance instead of wasting time stuck in destructive habits and painful emotions.

Initial Thoughts	Reactions	Corrective Action
1. Danger and Fear	Stress	
2. Indecision and Passivity	Procrastination	
3. Self-Doubt and Self-Criticism	Overwhelmed	
4. Past or Future	Anxiety	

Under pressure—when push comes to shove—you will react from your inherited survival functions that include the fight-or-flight stress response of the reptilian brain and the yielding or lowering response of the mammalian brain. These primitive survival mechanisms can be overridden when the human brain plays its proper leadership role in communicating that it is safe to release muscle tension and exhale and that your worth as a person is equal to that of a top dog superior. When you give yourself messages of safety and worth, the fear response will subside within seconds, and you can hold your head up high instead of bowing in submission or shame.

Replace Old Patterns with Corrective Action

Operating from a more effective management perspective, you now can catch the early symptoms of stress and quickly give yourself the messages of safety, choice, focus on the task, and presence that turn stress into success and make you a peak performer.

Initial Thoughts	Reactions	Corrective Action
1. Danger and Fear	Stress	SAFETY
2. Indecision and Passivity	Procrastination	CHOICE and EMPOWERMENT
3. Self-Doubt and Self-Criticism	Overwhelmed	TASK-ORIENTED FOCUS
4. Past or Future	Anxiety	PRESENCE

Taking corrective action is associated with human brain leadership functions that put you in charge of deciding what to do after your initial reactions.

A Plan for Survival Shuts off Worry

The worrying voice repeats, "What if I fail? What if I can't finish on time? What if they don't like my work?" Worrying is your brain's way of asking: What's your plan for survival? You do have a plan, don't you? How many times do I have to wake you up at 3 AM before you start making a plan? Do you think you can still use that old plan from 20 years ago?

While the worrying voice could be blamed for keeping you from enjoying a good night's sleep, it's just doing its job of reminding you of the need for a plan to survive situations that you've labeled as dangerous. The mind's "what if?" voice is also asking for some activity—such as cleaning up the spilled milk—that is more effective than your old, outdated methods of trying to avoid the situation by blaming yourself or trying to answer "Why does this always happen to me?" Being effective for the long haul requires that you adapt to the situation with action plans that address the current environment with your current skill set and adult intellect, not the outdated, limited coping ability you had in childhood.

This is where your superior leadership skills come into play in maintaining a clear focus on your mission, making a risk-benefit analysis, and rapidly shifting to your plan for recovery from setbacks. Your plan for survival and maintenance of a solid sense of worth regardless of what happens answers the "what if" questions and quiets that survival function. It says, in effect:

> This is what I will do if that happens. Here's the plan for rapidly recovering without suffering weeks of procrastination and shame. And by the way, your worth is safe with me. I won't allow anyone to determine your worth. Regardless of what anyone says, I will not make you feel bad.

Answering Your Worrying Mind

Your worrying mind needs answers to its "what if" questions. Stop trying to ignore its questions or dismiss them with "it's okay. You don't have to worry." Your worrying mind won't buy that. It doesn't feel okay. It's scared and wants a realistic plan. Set aside a few minutes to answer the "what if" questions with a plan that says "This is what we'll do if that happens." Instead of trying to ignore them, do a mental rehearsal of how to face and deal with your worst fears and most persistent worries.

For example,

Worrying mind: "What if you lose this angry customer?"

You: "At first, I'd feel awful. My first reaction would be anxiety about losing income and harming my reputation with my boss.

Then I'd draft a letter of apology and request more information to see what I can do to win her back.

I could ask my coworker to review the letter, and ask if I should call or send an e-mail.

Then I'd feel good that at least I'd faced my fears, stopped procrastinating, and did what I could to address and possibly correct the problem."

When the worrying mind keeps asking you "what if" questions, pay attention and start answering, "This is what I would do if that happens." If the questions persist, do a *realistic*—not a falsely positive—mental rehearsal of what you'd experience, how you'd react, who you'd call for help, what you'd do, and how you'd feel after completing your plans.

What would you experience physically and emotionally if that [put your worry here] happened?

_____

_____

How would you react if it really happened?

_____

_____

Who would you call for help?

_____

_____

What would you do next?

_____

_____

How would you feel after you survived the crisis? How would you forgive yourself for being vulnerable to loss and accept yourself as a normal human being?

_____

_____

Remember that self-acceptance, regardless of what happens, is the ultimate plan that quiets the worrying mind.

Mental Rehearsal for Coping with Personnel Worries

What if there are recurring problems with certain team members, customers, suppliers, or competitive coworkers and supervisors? How would you typically react when something or someone goes wrong, causing delays in the timely completion of your project? Which people are the most likely to trigger a counterproductive reaction from you? Do a mental rehearsal to become aware of your usual reactions and what you must do to access your superior, more effective relationship skills.

Which default reactions can you expect? Would you feel self-righteous in venting your anger? Would open expression of your initial feelings clear the air or lessen your authority?

_____

_____

For how long would you be angry, upset, and lose sleep? Which skills can you use to calm your reactions and emotions so you can act effectively?

_____

_____

Would you let your anger and frustration affect your life at home and your attitude with friends and family? What can you do to keep your home and personal life as a separate place from the stresses of work?

_____

_____

Which of your usual reactions will alert you to switch to effective ways of communicating with another person? What reactions will remind you to stay focused on quickly resolving your upset and the problem?

_____

_____

How will you stop insisting you're right so you can hear the other person and resolve the conflict? Would you rather be acknowledged for being right on the issue or for being effective in solving the problem?

_____

_____

Prepare for Ego Rebellion

Do you ever wonder why you can be successful at changing a negative habit or starting a healthy one, only to find that after 30 or 60 days you're back to your old ways? One possible answer is that your old way of coping feels unemployed, fired, and displaced by your leadership. It wants its old job back, and it doesn't understand how these new methods are working so easily for you while it's on the sidelines. Your old habit was working adequately for decades, as long as it had its security blankets of procrastination, overeating, drinking, checking e-mail, and other distractions to help it continue its inefficient struggle of trying to drive faster in first gear.

But you've discovered a better, more relaxed creative process, one that uses more of your brain and subconscious resources as part of your team approach to problem solving.

Your old ego or habit wants to return to the old ways of struggling as if separate from the rest of your brain. It doesn't want you to use structures and techniques that speed your work and allow you to shift into overdrive. It loves to struggle in first gear and put in extra hours to prove that it's using its consciously controlled muscles to work hard.

As you become a more effective self-leader, you will be changing the job description of those parts of you that have been running your life while you were absent or asleep. They will see this change as a demotion or a firing and will struggle to maintain control by offering you your usual distractions and favorites.

If you've been in the habit of delegating control of your life to primitive survival functions, they will insist that you need them and that you should not use your new tools. Even though

and perhaps because you are working more easily and creatively without struggle and procrastination, your old habits
will tap you on the shoulder and ask: "Are you sure this is
working? Don't you miss our good old days of struggling alone
without needing the crutch of your subconscious genius?"

Be prepared to give your ego and its old habits a new job
description that involves working as part of a team with your
larger brain and your new leadership. Otherwise, after weeks of
progress, you may be tempted to abandon these new tools and
slip back into old ways of struggling, as if your identity is
represented by only a small part of your brain over your left ear.
You now have ways of incorporating more of your brain and
even your subconscious wisdom and right-brain perspective.

A Word of Support

Enjoy making progress on your unique journey to becoming a
more effective manager of yourself and others. You can expect
to break through former obstacles more quickly and to experience higher levels of productivity as you access new skills and
your own deeper resources.

Your job as a businessperson or an entrepreneur can be a
lonely one in which most of the decisions and responsibilities
must rest with you. In this *Now Habit at Work* program, the
sense of who *you* are has expanded to include more of your
brain power and internal resources so that no part of you needs
to struggle alone.

No great project is accomplished alone. No treacherous
challenge is surmounted alone.

No great institution is governed from one lone perspective.
As an effective leader, your job is to integrate your support and

internal forces so that "I" now means an integrated team in which all parts of you are emboldened by your leadership vision. While parts of you may never feel completely confident or know how to survive through difficult times, now there is an effective leader whose vision and commitment to higher values unite all parts into an effective team.

As the one in charge of your life, you now have at your fingertips a powerful set of tools for achieving success in business: time and life management skills; the language of effective self-management; effective communication; the power of focusing; the power of a compelling mission; ignited motivation; effective goal setting; and skills in managing procrastinators and difficult employees. Now the real work begins: applying these tools and strategies every day to your work and your life.

With these tools, you have access to unusual and dynamic solutions to the problems that keep so many businesspeople from achieving a personal best performance, optimizing their talents, and reaching their goals. Use this book as your strategic planner for ongoing success in your future. When your old self lacks confidence, think of Wayne Gretzky encouraging you to take a shot, and use what you've learned here about accessing and applying your new skills.

You don't have to wait to feel confident or motivated. Simply take that first step into the unknown to get started. Build on all steps in the right direction, and make note of your progress every 30 days to see how far you've come. You'll discover that when you take a step forward, your *Now Habit at Work* strategies will act like a motion detector, shining a light on the path to your success.

[For ongoing support, updates, and answers to FAQs see www.neilfiore.com *and* www.neilfiore.blogspot.com.*]*

Appendix

Simple Solutions to Complex Problems

This appendix provides brief summaries of key points.

Tips for Making More Time

Time is the most healing thing you can give yourself today.

- Give yourself one extra minute, or drop one last-minute chore, before starting your day. Take a 10-minute walk before collapsing in front of the TV or computer.
- When starting your car, take three deep breaths (about 15 seconds total) to think about where you're going and to ensure that no one is behind you before put your car in gear.
- Honor transitions between projects, calls, and customers with 6 to 12 deep breaths (30 to 60 seconds) as you let go of the last task and before you start on a new activity.
- Honor the Sabbath or Shabbat by having nothing scheduled and no to do list for at least 4 to 24 hours every weekend.
- Plan a 2-hour lunch with friends or colleagues every week or two.
- Give yourself an extra 30 minutes at the gym to stretch.
- Shut the television off early, and give yourself an hour to think about what went well today.

- Cut one "I have to" from today's to do list. In fact, why not cut "have to" from your vocabulary?
- Focus on just one thing for at least 15 minutes without interruption.
- Eliminate one stop in your mad dash to accomplish all your chores all at once.
- Look up. Notice the sky, the clouds, and the trees. Let your attention include something in this world that is larger and more real than your worries, fears, and pains.

Time Management and the Art of Balance

1. **Do the *right* work.** Decide what your bottom-line, top-priority work is—that is, what's most important, not merely urgent. Avoid the workaholic syndrome of continually putting out fires and working without priorities.

2. **Distinguish *ego-oriented* work from *task-oriented* work.** Defending your worth is usually unnecessary. Often 50 percent of some tasks can be eliminated by concentrating on what really has to be done to complete the task rather than trying to avoid criticism or prove that you deserve praise.

3. **Think *small*.** Rather than overwhelming yourself with the expectation of doing 60 hours of work—or even 8 hours—to *finish* the job, focus on when you can find just 30 minutes to *get started*. Ask yourself throughout the day: "When can I start for 15 to 30 minutes?"

4. ***Preprogram* your brain with solutions.** Each night and especially every Sunday evening, spend a few minutes seeding your mind with the top-priority task you'll start on the next day. When you're stuck, overwhelmed, or tired, take two to five minutes to brainstorm how the job might be tackled, divided up, delegated, or reduced. Get in your mind the specific time when you will start on a specific part of the project.

5. **Go from *overwhelm* to *overview*.** When you first approach a large task, your mind will call for enough energy to try to finish it all at once. Use this agitated level of energy to overview the entire task and back-time from the future deadline to the starting point. Assign start-lines instead of deadlines to doable segments of the task, leading back to when you will start today.

6. **Don't procrastinate on living.** You cannot put your life on hold. It will backfire, increase resistance to work, and reduce your efficiency and productivity. Remember to eat well, sleep, exercise, and make yourself leave the office for lunch, to walk, and to take a break.

7. **Keep the *big picture* in mind.** Insist on time for your life, your family, your church, your career, and your relationship with yourself. Avoid the temptation to get lost in trying to do more work. *Live now* the life you've always wanted—a few minutes each day, a few hours each weekend—to keep from burning out, resenting your work, and losing motivation.

From Overwhelmed to Overjoyed: Multitasking without Freaking Out

You will feel overwhelmed if you:

- Maintain the fantasy that you're superhuman and should be able to do it all and keep an impossible to do list. Normal human beings who are not gods can't do it all and must choose what to let go of in order to focus on top priorities.

- Use perfectionism in an attempt to avoid mistakes and criticism. No wonder you feel overwhelmed. Being perfect and trying to completely escape mistakes and criticism can't be done, and the attempt requires two to four times as much time and effort as just doing what the job requires within the deadline.

- Put your mind in the imaginary future by insisting, "I have to get all of this work *done*." Your body remains in the real present and can't get into the future, so its energy is stuck, leaving you feeling anxious.

- Take a two-dimensional view of projects—trying to leap to the finish line all at once—rather than seeing tasks spread out over distance and time with breaks and a clear image of where and when to start the race.

- Focus on self-criticism rather than the work of just doing the task. You ask yourself, "What's wrong with me? Why didn't I start on this sooner?" rather than "What does the task require? What do I know about this now? What can I accomplish in 10 to 30 minutes?"

Five Ways to Stop Feeling Overwhelmed by Multiple Projects

1. Anticipate the need to shift between two levels of energy:
   - *High energy* that can turn into high anxiety and even panic if you don't create a strategic overview, blueprint, or outline of your projects. This unproductive, explosive energy comes from trying to grasp the start, middle, and end of a project all at the same time. It's like throwing a match into a car's gas tank instead of igniting the spark plugs.
   - *Focused energy* to work on the details and steps, the level where you could get lost in the details by working without a sense of focus or deadlines, producing volumes of work that are not related to the goal and take you off target.

2. Spread out the whole project, or your multiple projects, like a map to see the path you will be taking over the next few days, weeks, or months. Know that you will become smarter, stronger, and more confident once you begin this journey. Stretch the condensed energy of the overwhelmed feeling over the entire length of the project instead of trying to jump to the deadline (or the end of the path or the top of the mountain) all at once. Focus on when and where to start, and your body will adjust your energy to the just right level to be productive.

3. Take ownership of your deadlines. Translate *their* deadlines into several intermediate deadlines that fit

your leisure and family schedule and your need for feedback on rough drafts. With your own personal deadlines in place, you have a more realistic feel for the project, and you'll have taken some control over your work schedule and created some breathing space between each step. This will give you a clearer image of the smaller, doable tasks and will minimize procrastination because you'll no longer feel as if your life is controlled by deadlines imposed by an external authority you must rebel against.

4. Take a break from your detail work every 30, 60, or 90 minutes to check your overview and ensure that you are on target and on deadline. By checking your overview, you'll feel less anxious about making a mistake or doing work that is not relevant to the current project. Now you can feel confident that your focused, detailed work contributes to the next step in accomplishing your larger mission.

5. Give yourself a strong sense of worth that is not available for others to judge. With a guarantee that you will not beat yourself up if something goes wrong, every part of you will relax and focus on just doing the job—one step at a time without feeling overwhelmed with anxiety.

By using these five steps, you'll soon be one of those people who easily shifts from a strategic plan to the details—rapidly handling large projects and multiple demands with grace and ease.

Expect a Surprise: Work Creatively

1. Expect a surprise. Ignite your curiosity about what you will learn in facing something you don't know how to do immediately. Let go of worrying and struggle with only your conscious mind and wonder what will come to you when you connect to the superior wisdom of your subconscious genius and right-brain hemisphere.

2. Tell yourself: "This is going to be interesting. Soon I'll know something I don't know yet." This is the essence of creativity—going from worry to wonder and watching your mind rapidly move you from not-knowing to knowing something you didn't know a few seconds ago. "I'm showing up expecting a surprise."

3. Get your procrastination inoculation shot. Start on the projects you tend to avoid several times a day for 5 to 30 minutes. Just getting started breaks inertia and moves you to momentum. Facing your most feared projects breaks the habit of procrastination and makes it easier for you to start next time.

4. Practice strategic cramming. Instead of worrying about *their* deadlines, create your own personal deadlines that take into account your plans, holidays, and your schedule.

5. See how quickly you can make a rough outline in 5 or 10 minutes, and decide if you can devote 5 to 10 hours to your top-priority project this week. Once ideas start

flowing, you'll feel excited about working rapidly and creatively. Then you can decide about investing another 10 hours the following week.

6. Remember how you felt when you helped a friend cope with a stressful or heartbreaking event. You may have the same problem, but you changed your perspective and played the role of a compassionate, wise friend. This helped you observe the problem from a distance and access your deep, creative problem-solving resources. Now do this for yourself and the part of you that is overwhelmed and stressed and doesn't know how to cope.

Hardy Executives

Executives possessing three hardiness characteristics—commitment, control, and challenge—can withstand stress and resist illness better than their peers who lack them, according to University of Chicago professor Suzanne Kobasa. That is, you can reduce the effects of change and stress in your life by taking charge of how you respond to everyday pressures.

In later research, she noted that those people with high stress scores who did not get sick shared some additional characteristics: a life plan with established priorities, a high level of self esteem, an internal sense of control, and an action orientation.

A closer look at these four characteristics reveals that the research supports your *Now Habit at Work* effective self-management strategies: create a leadership vision, make a risk-benefit analysis, run your life from your human brain, and focus on what you can do and let go of the rest. Professor Kobasa's research tells us that by living as a true leader, you will lessen stress and create resilience against illness. You don't have to be afraid of the normal, everyday stresses of life and business.

Here are those four characteristics integrated with *Now Habit at Work* strategies.

1. A life plan with established priorities

Develop a clear, compelling vision for each of the major areas of your life: work, family, personal health. Focus every day on a plan that tells you when you can start on your highest priorities at work, with family, and on your personal health and development. Let go of trying to do everything and to control everything and everybody. Focus on one top priority at a time for 15 to 30 minutes of uninterrupted work.

2. A high level of self esteem

Maintain self-worth and self-esteem regardless of what occurs in life and regardless of what others think or say. Acknowledge the laws and rituals of your culture, but oppose being lowered by them. Maintain your human ability to hold your head up high in spite of criticism. Do not allow your worth as a person to be judged.

3. An internal sense of control

Instead of blaming life and others, take responsibility for what you can control. Remember, you're human: You can't do everything, and you don't have responsibility for everything that happens. Focus on what you can do to make things better, and you will feel and be more effective.

4. An action orientation

Work on problem solving rather than wasting time on defending yourself against real or imagined criticism. Rather than seeking someone or something to blame, take the initiative to start corrective action.

Putting It into Action

Action Steps and Commitments

As an effective self-manager, you integrate all parts of your external and internal team to contribute to the compelling vision you've created. You also make a clear commitment to yourself, your organization, and your future.

Your Leadership Commitment

1. This is my life, my body, my career.

2. Certain beliefs, fears, habits, relationships, and addictions are toxic to the full functioning of my life, my body, and my career.

3. I'm committed to protecting my life, body, and career from all toxins. I'm committed to developing the full potential of my talents.

4. I will reduce stress, create inner peace, and speak to myself and my employees in the language of effective leadership: safety, choice, focus, and presence.

I will use techniques from Chapter ___ and Chapter ___.
I commit to using these techniques to: _____
_____
_____

I will start:
When [the specific time]: _____
Where: _____

What part of the project: _____

_____

Even if [list your favorite distractions—hunger, fatigue, lateness, e-mail]: _____

_____

I will follow up with a coworker or partner on:

Issue: _____

Date: _____

Time: _____

Frequency: _____

Index

Absenteeism, 122, 123
Action, shifting to from
    reaction, 11, 12, 160
Action steps, 81–83, 93, 94,
    96, 98, 113, 161, 162
Active listening, 47–53, 55,
    119, 120
Alessandra, Tony, 45
Anxiety, 6, 8, 18–20, 25, 31,
    34, 71, 93, 112, 136,
    138, 140, 141, 155, 156

Beliefs and expectations, 41,
    42, 84, 85, 133
Blanchard, Ken, 29, 38
*Blindsided: A Manager's Guide
    to Catastrophic Incidents
    in the Workplace* (Blythe),
    118
Blythe, Bruce, 118, 119

Carnegie, Dale, 38
Choice

attitude and behavior,
    changing, 35, 36, 136,
    141
fears and self-doubts,
    facing, 12
procrastinators,
    management of, 111, 112
shifting to from "have to"
    mindset, 6–8, 10, 11, 71,
    73, 75, 111, 112
Commitment, 21, 23, 35, 73,
    90, 103, 131, 135, 159,
    161, 162
Communication
differences, 56–59
difficult and violence-prone
    employees, 119–121
effective versus ineffective,
    47–49
exercise for, 51–53
guidelines for, 53–56
"I" statements, 54, 55, 120
and learning styles, 57, 59

Communication (*Continued*)
listening, 47–55, 59, 119–121
nonverbal, 40, 51–53
paraphrasing, 49–55, 121
styles of, 56–58
as tool for success, 148
Confucius, 15
Container Store, The, 123
Corrective action
and effectiveness, 3, 4, 12, 130, 131
shifting to from current habit, 3, 4, 12, 38, 71, 76, 130, 136, 140, 141, 160
Coworkers
attitude toward, 42
mental rehearsal for coping with, 144, 145
Creativity, 8, 9, 17, 42, 79, 133, 137, 157, 158
Crisis preparedness, 118
Customers
listening to, 47–50, 59, 119, 120. *See also* Listening
mental rehearsal for coping with, 144, 145
satisfaction, 122–124

Deadlines. *See* Time management

Decision making, 18
Depression, 6, 7, 31, 34, 41–43, 65, 80, 93, 136
Difficult employees, managing
challenging authority, reasons for, 115, 116
communication skills, 119–121
customers, treating employees like, 121, 122
employee satisfaction, improving, 122–124
negative attention, 117
positive incentives and recognition, 117, 118
respect for employees, 119, 121
as tool for success, 148
violence-prone employees, 118–121
Drucker, Peter F., 18

The Effective Executive (Drucker), 18
Effectiveness
communication. *See* Communication
and corrective action, 3, 4, 12, 76, 130, 131, 140, 141

language of effective
managers, applying, 139,
140
and self-management, 4, 8,
37–39, 42, 127–130, 148
support for achieving, 147,
148
theory, putting into
practice, 127–129
and time management,
17–19
Ego
rebellion, 146, 147
task focus, shifting to from
ego focus, 5, 6, 12, 152
80-20 rule. *See* Pareto
principle (80-20 rule)
Ekman, Paul, *40*
Ellis, Albert, 31
Emotional Intelligence
(Goleman), 88
Emotions Revealed:
Recognizing Faces and
Feelings to Improve
Communication and
Emotional Life (Ekman),
40
Employees
absenteeism, 122, 123
customers, treating like,
121, 122

difficult. *See* Difficult
employees, managing
job satisfaction, 122–124
respect for, 121
satisfaction, 122–124
training, 122–124
violent, 118–121
Escape plan, 32–35
Essential strategies for
optimal performance.
See Strategies for optimal
performance
Executive brain, 71, 72, 75

Failure, fear of, 83, 110, 111,
116, 141
Feedback, 18, 25–27, 114
Focus
focusing in one breath,
exercise for, 74, 75
importance of, 63, 64
improving, exercise for, 66,
67
mental toughness, 76
mission, 64, 66, 67, 71,
74–76, 142
task focus, shifting to from
ego focus, 5, 6
tips for achieving optimal
performance, 65
as tool for success, 148

Fortune magazine 100 Best
Companies to Work For,
122
Frankl, Viktor, 39, 40
Free time, 22, 23

Gardner, John, 69
Goals
action steps versus being
stuck, 98–101, 103
commitment, 102, 103,
131, 132, 135
dangers of goal setting, 93,
94
elements of effective goal
setting, 101–103
and focus, 64
functional goal, 102, 103
goal setting as tool for
success, 148
habits, changing, 95–97
language of effective
managers, 139, 140
long-term success,
rehearsing for, 131–133
quiz, 104, 105
realistic, 94, 95
setting as a process, 103
and subconscious, 103, 104
tips for setting, 97, 102
ultimate goal, 95, 102, 103

unrealistic, 94
Goleman, Daniel, 88
Goodnight, Jim, 121
Grafton, Sue, 19
Gretzky, Wayne, 125, 148

Habits
ego rebellion, preparing
for, 146, 147
and long-term success,
131–136
negative habits,
overcoming, 129–131
Hardiness characteristics,
159, 160
"Have to" mindset
choice, shifting to, 6–8, 10,
11, 152
inner dialogue, 138, 139
and mission, 71, 75
and procrastination, 110
result of, 154
and self-management, 35,
44
and time management, 20,
28

"I" statements, 54, 55, 120
Illness, ability to resist, 122,
159, 160
Inner dialogue

and "have to" mindset, 28, 31, 138, 139
language of effective managers, 139, 140
procrastinators, 110, 111
and self-management, 31, 35–38, 41

Kobasa, Suzanne, 159

Leadership commitment, 73, 161, 162
Learning styles, 57, 59
Leonard, Elmore, 19
Life plan, 159, 160
Listening. *See also* Communication
active listening, 47–53, 55, 119, 120
and paraphrasing, 49–55, 121
Lombardi, Vince, 61

Madden, John, 57
Man's Search for Meaning (Frankl), 39
McGregor, Douglas, 36
Mission
and focus, 64, 66, 67, 71, 74–76, 142
statements, drafting, 73

statements, examples of, 71, 72
as tool for success, 148
Motivation
external rewards, 79
internal, 79
lack of, 87, 88
marshmallow study, 88
ownership, 80, 85, 86
pain, avoidance of, 80, 81
positive expectancy, 80–85
and success in achieving goals, 80
tips for getting motivated, 89, 90
as tool for success, 148
Multitasking, 17, 154–156

The One Minute Manager (Blanchard), 29, 38
Optimism, 42
Overwhelmed feeling, 10, 17, 20, 23–25, 44, 93, 97, 103, 110, 111, 138, 140, 141, 153–156, 158

Pareto principle (80-20 rule), 89
Perfectionism, 18, 21, 26, 27, 65, 111, 113, 114, 133, 137, 154

Personal life, 21, 145, 159, 160
Personality styles, 56–58
Pessimism, 42
Plan for survival, 141, 142
Priorities
  getting started, 18–20, 39
  goal setting, 97, 104, 105
  and life plan, 159, 160
  and time management, 21–25, 71, 72, 152, 153
Procrastination
  counterproductive self-talk, 110, 111
  management of procrastinators, 109–115
  reasons for, 110, 111
  and time management, 17, 18, 20, 22, 23
  tips for overcoming, 157, 158

Recurring problems, rehearsing response to, 144, 145
Reverse effort (shifting from struggle to ease), 4, 5

SAS (Business Analytic Solutions), 121, 122

Self-acceptance, 113, 114, 144
Self-criticism, 6, 31, 43, 44, 65, 74, 110, 132, 133, 135, 154
Self-esteem, 26, 42, 93, 94, 116, 120, 133, 159–160
Self-management
  and ability to withstand stress and resist illness, 159, 160
  actions versus words, 39, 40
  attitude and behavior changes, 35, 36, 40–42
  catch yourself doing something right, 38
  choosing what not to do, 38, 39
  escape plan, 34, 35
  and job dissatisfaction, 33, 34
  metamessages, 40–43
  push or pull motivation, 36, 37
  reality, choosing, 32, 33
  and self-criticism, 31, 32
  and stress-survival response, 43, 44
  tips for, 43
  as tool for success, 148

"why" versus "how"
      questioning, 37, 38
Self-talk. *See* Inner dialogue
Seligman, Martin, 42
Setbacks
   and focus, 64, 76
   and goals, 95, 102, 131
   recovering from, 43, 133,
      135–138, 142
   resiliency, building,
      133–135
Sleep
   habits, changing, 96, 97
   importance of, 9, 17, 104,
      153
   lack of, 34, 80, 133, 141,
      145
Starting
   immediately, 18, 19
   keep starting versus
      finishing, 19, 20
   procrastinators,
      management of, 112–113
   shifting to from finishing, 8
Strategies for optimal
      performance, 3–13, 148
Stress. *See also* Anxiety;
      Worry
   effects of, 34, 80, 122
   reducing, 9, 65, 66, 71–73,
      129, 134, 141, 159, 161

response, 43, 44, 138, 140
   and self-talk, 36, 43, 44
Subconscious, shifting to
      from conscious mind,
      9–11, 157
Success, long-term
   rehearsing for, 131–133
   setbacks, dealing with,
      133–138
Supervisors
   mental rehearsal for coping
      with, 144, 145
   support of, 123
Survival plan, 141–144. *See
      also* "What if" questions

Task focus
   procrastinators,
      management of, 111
   shifting to from ego focus,
      5–7, 12
Theory X and Theory Y
      (McGregor), 36
Time management
   and balance, 152, 153
   commitments, scheduling,
      23
   deadlines, 17–20, 24–27
   to do lists, 18–23
   feedback and overcoming
      perfectionism, 18, 26, 27

Time (*Continued*)
  multitasking, 17, 154–156
  procrastination, 17, 18, 20,
    22, 23
  starting, 18, 19
  time limits, setting, 17,
    18
  tips for, 20, 23, 25, 27–28,
    151, 152
Tindell, Kip, 123
To do list, managing
  alternative lists, 21–23
  and "have to" mindset,
    19–21
  priorities, 20–22
  tips for, 20
Townsend, Robert, 1

Victim mindset, 7, 35, 110,
  111, 119
Violence-prone employees,
  118–121

Wainwright, Don, 122
Wainwright Industries, 122
"What if" questions, 12, 72,
    127, 141–143. *See also*
    Worry
"Why" versus "how"
    questioning
  and self-management, 37,
    38
  and shift from current habit
    to corrective action, 3, 4
Wilson, Colin, 91
Workaholism, 17, 21, 109,
    152
Worry, 19, 20, 72, 74,
    110–112, 127, 133, 138,
    140–145, 152, 157. *See
    also* Anxiety; "What if"
    questions
www.neilfiore.blogspot.com,
    148
www.neilfiore.com, 148